All About
Action Photography

All About
Action Photography

DAVID HODGSON

PELHAM BOOKS · LONDON

First published in Great Britain by
PELHAM BOOKS LIMITED
52 Bedford Square
London, WC1B 3EF
March 1976
Second Impression April 1978

© 1976 by David Hodgson

ISBN 0 7207 0888 5

Filmset in eleven on twelve point Plantin
and printed by
BAS Printers Limited, Over Wallop, Hampshire

Contents

Introduction

An action photograph makes a unique visual statement. It lays bare for us the mystery of movement and allows us to explore a world of speeds too fast for the naked eye to analyse. Only with a camera can we transfix time; freeze the beating of a humming bird's wings; capture the gravity-defying leap of an athlete or the explosive forces of destruction as a racing car spins from the track.

Because of this extraordinary power to let us not only see but leisurely inspect each detail of the otherwise unseeable, action pictures are probably the most dramatically eye-catching of all photographs.

Many photographers hesitate to shoot action because they feel it must present extraordinary difficulties or demand expensive and specialised equipment. Neither of these widely held assumptions is correct, as I shall hope to show in the following pages.

It is true, however, that taking successful action photographs presents the photographer with problems which are not found in other branches of picture taking. The landscape and portrait specialist, for example, can exercise a high degree of control over his subjects both before and, sometimes, during the shooting session. The pictorialist can carefully select his viewpoint to achieve the best possible composition, choose a time of year and day when the light gives him exactly the effect he wants and, using a tripod, expose his film at the shutter speed and f-stop combination he judges will produce the finest result. The portrait photographer has much the same sort of control over his pictures, while the lucky glamour photographer can even pick and choose his subjects. The action photographer is much less the captain of his own fate. Before the action starts he may have little chance to exercise any control. His camera angles may be dictated by officials, regulations and sometimes the need to preserve his own neck! His exposure will often be determined by the need to use a fast shutter speed; his depth of field by the necessity of using a long focal length lens in order to bring the action in close. Once the action has started he must shoot and hope for the best. Often he has no real idea how good, or how bad, his pictures will be until the film is processed. If he has failed it is usually impossible to ask for a re-shoot. Neither the racing driver who has spun off the track nor the boxer who has been knocked out for the count are likely to repeat the experience for his benefit! If the action isn't in the camera the first time it never will be.

This seeming uncertainty, coupled with the technical problems of focusing accurately on fast-moving objects and timing the shots correctly when a hairbreadth hesitation in releasing the shutter may spell the difference between success and failure, is enough to deter many photographers from action work.

This is a pity because, apart from producing exciting pictures, there is no more interesting, demanding and rewarding branch of photography. The moment of anticipation as you hold a length of newly processed film up to the light to discover whether or not the fates have been kind to you is a never ending thrill. If you have succeeded in snatching a first-class action shot under difficult conditions, then the deep glow of satisfaction and sense of achievement makes all the difficulties seem unimportant. To shoot good action pictures under all sorts of conditions you must learn new skills and brush up existing techniques. If you have a simple, inexpensive camera then action work is still possible but you must learn to use your camera within its limitations in order to achieve the best results. In the following pages I shall describe how you can master these techniques quickly and easily to become a very proficient action photographer.

There is a bonus to be had for learning these special skills. Although they are designed to make you a good action photographer, they will also improve your picture-taking technique in every other branch of photography. You will gain speed, certainty and confidence, acquiring the ability to use your camera quickly and effectively in the only way it should ever be used . . . as an extension of your seeing eye.

THE ILLUSTRATIONS AND HOW TO USE THEM

This book contains over 100 photographs. Although each one has been used to illustrate some specific point, you should use them in a much wider context as well. Study each photograph carefully, in relation to the following six points.

1 *Composition*: Note the main lines of the composition. It may be helpful to draw out the key elements in each picture in a simplified form on a sheet of paper. Discover how frequently a *diagonal* line is used to convey a feeling of movement and speed in the pictures. When a diagonal line has not been used, assess what other factors, if any, in the picture convey action and unrest. Use two L-shaped pieces of card to mask the photographs and see if you can improve on them by this editing technique. See, for example, if the picture becomes more dramatic when the foreground and background areas are reduced; or if a change in the angle of the picture increases or decreases the feeling of movement.

2 *Camera Angle*: Note the viewpoint from which the picture was taken. This camera angle may have been dictated to the photographer by a variety of factors, or simply by chance. Put yourself in his position and see if a change of viewpoint—a lower or higher angle, for example—would have improved or harmed the picture.

3 *Lens Used :* In most cases it will be easy enough to see if the lens was a long focal length – the perspective will be compressed – or a wide angle – the increased depth of field will result in an over-all sharpness. Here again, the photographer may not have had any choice over the lens he used; it may simply be that he only had one lens. But try and decide if you would have used the same lens or a different one and consider how this change in lens would have affected the finished result.

4 *Background :* Do you find the background distracting? If so, it has probably reduced the impact of the picture. If the background is neutral, then note the technique which has been used to render it unobtrusive. Has the photographer put it out of focus, or blurred it, or what?

5 *Tonal Contrast :* If the picture makes a bold, dramatic and easy to understand statement, one of the key elements will be tonal contrast, especially contrast between the foreground subjects and the background, camera position, the use of lighting and so on.

6 *Timing :* This is harder to assess because, in many of the photographs, it will be impossible to tell whether a better picture could have been taken split seconds before or after the moment when the cameraman actually pressed the shutter release. One guide will be the expressions on the faces of any people involved. As I shall explain, expressions are a powerful element in conveying action in a still photograph. Expressions change rapidly, especially when people are involved in some fast-moving activity. Note how expressions can convey a feeling of effort, speed and movement. Where inanimate objects are concerned, note whether an earlier shutter release or a slight delay would have made the movement more or less dramatic. Where motorised sequences are printed, study each frame carefully, bearing in mind all the six points which I have outlined. Decide, in terms of composition, camera angle, lens, background, tonal contrast and timing, which photograph would make the best individual shot.

These photographs have been selected from thousands of possible action pictures not merely to make the book look more attractive or to break up the pages of print, nor even to point up a single simple fact from the text. They, as much as the words which I have written, will provide you with the key to successful action photography.

TECHNICAL TERMS

If your photographic experience is limited, some of the terms used may be unfamiliar. To avoid slowing down the text with detailed descriptions of basic terms, I have included a full explanation in the technical glossary at the back of the book.

PART ONE

CHAPTER ONE

Your Camera and Action Photography

Simple cameras

Into this category come all types of cameras which have the following:

a Non-interchangeable lenses.

b Shutter speeds of up to 1/300th second.

It might seem that the slow top shutter speed is going to be the most serious limitation for action work. But while it is true that some fast movement needs a very fast shutter speed – 1/1000th second, for example – to freeze it, this is not a critical problem. In Chapter Three I shall describe techniques by which you can take successful action pictures at slow shutter speeds. Indeed, some subjects look *more* dramatic when taken at such speeds.

PLATE 1
Action shots like this can be taken with simple cameras. Panning the camera with the movement has enabled fast action to be frozen at 1/125th second. The slight blur helps to convey a sense of speed

The more serious limitation is having a fixed *focal length* lens; usually a standard or slightly *wide angle* lens. In many cases it is impractical, impossible or just too dangerous to take the camera physically close to the subject. Under these circumstances a telephoto or long focal length lens must be fitted to produce a sufficiently large image on the negative.

By enlarging a portion of a negative you can, of course, pull up small parts of the image. But the optical quality of inexpensive lenses is not usually high enough to allow great enlargement. The definition falls off sharply and the print often looks disappointingly fuzzy. To make matters worse, action photography often involves you in increased development times and *fast films* (see Chapter Five). These combine to increase *grain size* and put another limitation on the extent to which a negative can be successfully enlarged. To get the best results with simple cameras I suggest that, in addition to following the procedures set down in Chapter Three, you:

1   Work as close to the subject as possible. As a guide, do not attempt to photograph any action which takes place more than 25 ft. away on a dull day when you are working near full aperture.

2   On a bright day, when you can use f8 or f11 (lens definition tends to be best at these f-stops) together with a slow film (for example, Ilford FP4 or Kodak Plus-X), it may be possible to take pictures of subjects up to 45 ft. away and obtain satisfactory enlargements.

3   Centre the subject in the viewfinder so that the picture is taken on the centre of the negative area. The definition of a lens is always best at its centre but may fall away sharply towards the edges.

Low-priced automatic cameras
Generally, these have the limitations of a fixed focal length lens which have been described above. Some, however, have a faster top shutter speed than 1/300th second. Such cameras can be quite helpful to beginners in action photography because they take care of the technical problems of exposure and allow you to concentrate your attention where it belongs – on the subject. There are some situations, however, where completely automatic cameras can be 'fooled' into under-exposing the main part of the picture. This may happen when shooting against sunlight or against the sky. For example, if you took a low angle picture of a high jump, the camera meter would read all the light coming from the sky and all the light being reflected by the subject and average out an exposure. Because so much back lighting was reaching the meter it might stop down the lens too much so that the image of the high-jumper was under-exposed. The same thing could happen if you were photographing two footballers leaping for a high ball. The players, the main point of interest in your picture, could be lacking in detail. There

are two ways of overcoming this problem. Some automatic cameras have a device which enables you to 'lock-in' an exposure after taking the meter reading. With such cameras you may be able to go in close to the subject, make a reading and then step back to the camera-taking position after locking that reading into your camera. Alternatively, where it is impossible to move in close to the subject – for example, at a football match they would not thank you for running on to the pitch to take a light reading off the players – you can take a reading off your hand. Hold your hand about 3 ft. from the camera to make the reading. Now lock this into the camera. If the light changes you will, of course, have to take a fresh reading. By measuring the light reflected from your hand you will ensure that flesh tones are rendered correctly.

If your camera is fully automatic, with no over-ride and no way of locking-in an exposure, strongly back-lit subjects are going to pose problems and you may always find them slightly under-exposed in the main subject areas. Films have a great deal of *exposure latitude* and

PLATES 2–5 (below and overleaf)
A sequence taken with a low-priced automatic camera. Shutter speed 1/300th second. Aperture f11. With this type of subject care must be taken to ensure that the large reflecting area of water does not produce under-exposure in the main part of the subject by 'fooling' the meter

careful printing may save them, but if you are using black and white stock there is a simple technique which can improve back-lit shots and make it easier to get good quality prints from the negative. This involves 'fooling' the meter so that it always slightly over-exposes the pictures. You do this by setting a lower speed rating on the film adjustment dial than you are actually using in the camera. Suppose, for example, you are using Kodak Tri-X film which is rated at 400 ASA. Instead of setting 400 ASA in the camera, set 160 ASA. Your normally-lit shots will now be slightly over-exposed, but your back-lit shots will have far greater detail. When making a print, it is easier to get a good result from a slightly dense negative than from one in which an important part of the image is under-exposed and lacking in detail.

But I do not advise you to use this technique when shooting colour transparencies because exposures are far more critical with this type of film.

35 mm. cameras – Range-finder

Into this category come all cameras with speeds up to 1/500th or 1/2000th second, interchangeable lenses and focusing by means of coupled range-finders. Perhaps the best known professional 35 mm. range-finder camera is the Leica. These cameras are quieter in operation than the single-lens reflex with its moving mirror, and many photographers find the split-image focusing and bright viewfinder easier to work with under low light levels. This makes them suitable for action work in theatres, nightclubs, circuses and so on. But when they are used in conjunction with long lenses the viewing is less certain and the composition harder than with an SLR. Leica make a reflex viewing finder – the Visoflex – to overcome this problem, but it is not as satisfactory as using an SLR to start with. A separate viewfinder or frame finder is usually necessary for very long lenses. Alternatively, it may be possible to fit reduction masks on the camera finder.

35 mm. cameras – Single-lens reflex

This is probably the most popular type of camera, both with amateurs and professionals, currently on the market. Viewing is through the taking lens via a mirror and pentaprism. When the shutter is released the mirror flips out of the way and then, in most designs, returns to the

PLATE 6
The range-finder camera is especially useful for action shots under low light levels. Leica camera 90 mm. lens 1/500th second f1.4. Tri-X rated to 1000 ASA (see Chapter Five)

viewing position as soon as the picture has been taken. For action photography it is important that the camera does have this 'instant return mirror' facility or the operation becomes slow and sequence work is made difficult. With an SLR, composition and focusing are easy and positive, although some difficulty may be experienced when using manual lenses (see Chapter Two) at small stops, or long lenses at low light levels. For action photographs the easiest type of screen to use in the viewfinder is probably one which incorporates a split-image finder in the centre. Many types of SLR now accept a motor-drive for fast sequence photography (see Chapter Seven) and when using a motor on a 35 mm. camera, up to 9 frames per second can be shot. The motor also enables the camera to be used by remote control at a considerable distance. This can be invaluable for obtaining different angles on action subjects.

Most SLR's now use a bayonet locking system for fitting

PLATE 7
An SLR is quick and easy to use under difficult conditions. Nikon F camera with 400 mm. Novoflex lens was used to capture this moment of agony in the life of a bull-fighter. 1/1000th second f11

interchangeable lenses. This is definitely preferable to the earlier screw locking system which was not only slower in use but, when working fast, there was always the risk of crossing the thread and jamming the lens. One difficulty found on SLR's, and all cameras using focal plane shutters, is the slow speed at which electronic flash has to be synchronised. This will be discussed at length in Chapter Six.

Single-lens reflex – 6 cm. × 6 cm. and 6 cm. × 7 cm. format
These cameras work on the same principle as 35 mm. SLR's, although some designs do not incorporate an instant-return mirror. The standard viewfinder is usually at waist-level, although pentaprism viewers can be added. The two best known 6 cm. × 6 cm. SLR's are the Swedish Hasselblad 500CM and the Japanese Bronica EC. Both are well designed and made, but they are quite bulky and very expensive. On the other hand, the large negative format does produce high-quality results.

The Hasselblad is fitted with a Compur (between-the-lens) shutter giving a top speed of 1/500th second. The Bronica has a focal plane shutter with a top speed of 1/1000th second. This makes the Bronica

PLATE 8
A Hasselblad 500EL fitted with a 250 mm. Sonnar lens was used to take this picture of a stunt motor-cyclist crashing through a blazing fence. 1/500th second f8

slightly more convenient for action photography than the Hasselblad, although there are some action subjects (which have to be recorded by flash) where the higher synchronisation speed of the Hasselblad is of great value (see Chapter Six). A second advantage of the Bronica's focal plane shutter is that the camera can be fitted with a wider range of non-standard lenses. It is possible to buy ex-ministry long focal length lenses far more cheaply than their modern counterparts. By having a suitable adaptor machined, such lenses may be fitted to the Bronica but, because the Hasselblad relies on a between-the-lens shutter to make the exposure, they cannot be used with this camera. An early version of the Hasselblad (the 1000F) had a focal plane shutter and these cameras can still be bought second-hand, although they went out of production many years ago. Although they were advanced for their time, and built to the high standard of design and manufacture which goes into all Hasselblad equipment, I do not recommend buying one second-hand as it is not reliable enough for hard, serious work. Both the Hasselblad 500C and the Bronica are versatile and give a very high-quality result, but again I would not advise you to buy either of these cameras if you intend to specialise in action photography. They are bulky, heavy and expensive. Unless you intend to use them with a wide range of lenses and film magazines (which are also very expensive) you will be paying for facilities which you do not sufficiently exploit.

Before leaving this type of camera I should mention the Hasselblad EL. This looks quite like the conventional Hasselblad, but instead of the film being wound on manually it is turned through the camera by an electric motor. This system should not be confused with 35 mm. motor-drives, however. These, as we shall see, are capable of taking sequence pictures at up to 9 frames per second. The Hasselblad EL takes one complete second to make an exposure and wind on the film. Although it has many valuable uses in the studio and scientific laboratory, sequence action and high-speed photography are not amongst them.

Twin-lens reflex camera—6 cm. × 6 cm. (non-interchangeable lens)
These are fitted with between-the-lens *Compur shutters* giving a top speed of 1/500th second. This limits the range of action subjects they can cover satisfactorily, although a high flash synchronisation speed can be useful. More serious than this, however, are the limitations imposed by the non-interchangeable lenses. Although it is possible to buy a Rolleiflex TLR camera with a fixed lens of longer than normal focal length, and cameras fitted with standard lenses can have their focal lengths increased by fitting additional lenses in front of them, neither device is much help to the sports and action photographer as a great deal of action photography needs to be taken with lenses of 240 mm. focal

PLATE 9
A Rolleiflex TLR was used to take this shot. With a high quality lens considerable enlargement is possible from the 6 cm. × 6 cm. negative format. 1/500th second f11

length and longer. The chief advantage which the owner of a high-quality fixed lens TLR has over the owner of a cheaper fixed focal length lens camera is the very high quality of the optical systems. These allow far greater enlargement without loss of definition. In this respect the TLR is far superior to the simple camera.

Some TLR's have a system whereby their viewfinder hoods can be quickly adapted into a frame 'sports finder'. On the Rollei, for example, the inside front section of the viewfinder hood is fitted with a mirror. This oblong is pushed down to produce a forward viewing frame, and the mirror comes to rest at an angle above the screen. By looking through a magnifier in the back of the hood, the photographer can quickly focus on the reflex screen, and then transfer the eye to a second viewing hole to use the frame finder. Certainly when using a TLR for action work some kind of frame finder is essential. The mirror system reverses the image on the screen from left to right, making it extremely difficult to pan the camera to follow a fast-moving subject. If you have a TLR which lacks a frame-finder facility and intend to use it for action

photography, I would advise you either to buy one or to make one up.

PLATE 10
The tele-lens on an interchangeable TLR camera enables you to get in just that useful bit closer to dangerous subjects. Mamyiaflex fitted with tele-lens and pull up from negative when printed adds impact to the picture. 1/500th second f5.6. 180 mm. lens

Twin-lens reflex cameras (interchangeable lenses)
This is the same type of camera as above, but the lenses are interchangeable. Probably the best-known camera of this type is the Mamyiaflex. By fitting the longer lenses available, you can overcome some of the problems of getting in close – though not all of them, due to the limited length of the longest focal length lens in the system – but you still have the problem of a relatively slow top shutter speed (1/500th second). Furthermore, the camera is rather bulky and slow to use compared with a 35 mm.

Press cameras
These are usually large format cameras (a 5 in. × 4 in. negative was standard in Fleet Street for many years) which take sheet film or plates in *dark slides*. They can also be used with roll-film backs taking 120 film.

PLATE 11
Good quality can be obtained from the large format press camera negatives. But note how static this completely 'frozen' shot of a stock car crash looks. Blur can add impact. MPP press camera fitted with roll-film back. 1/2000th second f16. 150 mm. lens on 6 cm. × 9 cm. format

They are usually fitted with two different types of shutter. There is a between-the-lens Compur shutter with a top speed of 1/500th second and a focal plane shutter built in to the body of the camera. This may have a top speed of 1/2000th second or more. The speed of the blind shutter is varied in two ways. Firstly, by increasing or decreasing the tension of the blind spring and, secondly, by varying the split between the two blinds. The narrower the slit the faster the shutter speed. When using a shutter on some types of high-speed action — for example, to freeze racing cars — you can get a curious form of distortion which results in the cars having oval wheels. This is because the cars have moved a fraction during the time it has taken the roller blind to travel across the negative. On old pictures of cars, motor bikes and so on, you will frequently see this odd effect. Press cameras usually focus in two ways. There is a ground-glass screen at the back. When both shutters are opened it is possible to focus and compose on this screen. For action work the camera is provided with a frame finder and a coupled range-finder. These cameras are heavy and slow in operation. Even when fitted with a roll-film holder they take an experienced operator a second or so to wind on the film and reset the shutter.

Furthermore, because of the long focal length of the standard lens, depth of field is limited. Frequently the maximum aperture of their lenses is fairly small (typically f4.5 or f5.6) which makes them difficult to use in poor light. Despite all these disadvantages they can be very useful in action photography. They employ a large negative format, even when used with a roll-film holder, and this means high-quality enlargements. The frame finder is fast and easy to use. They combine the advantages of a high-speed focal plane shutter with a between-the-lens shutter that enables you to take electronic flash pictures at a high speed (see Chapter Six). The focal plane shutter means that they can be used with a variety of low-priced ex-ministry lenses. They can be bought very reasonably second-hand and, as they are tough and will stand up to a lot of rough treatment, they are a less risky second-hand buy than more fragile and sophisticated equipment. If you are thinking of starting action photography on a limited budget then I advise you to seriously consider buying a Speed Graphic or MPP. They are difficult cameras to use well, but once you have mastered them you will find the transfer to a miniature camera very easy. It's a bit like learning to drive on a truck with a non-synchromesh gear box. The lessons may be hard but once you can drive that sort of vehicle you can handle anything. Although it is impossible to quote prices because they change so rapidly these days, as a guide you should be able to buy a good second-hand press camera with a range of lenses for about the price of a quality second-hand 35 mm. SLR body. But make sure the camera has with it, or can be fitted with, a roll-film holder. Otherwise you will be shooting all your pictures on 5 in. × 4 in. sheet film which will cost a not so small fortune!

One final advantage of the press camera: as a photo-journalist who trained on such equipment, I can testify that a Speed Graphic, together with its leather case and a dozen double-dark slides, is one of the finest crowd-parters ever designed. Swing a press camera around and people don't stand to argue. They shift. As an added bonus you will look so much like everybody's concept of what a press photographer should look like that you may find previously closed doors flung open to you!

AT A GLANCE CAMERA CHECK CHART

Simple Cameras

This group comprises all cameras which have a fixed (non-interchangeable) focal length lens, including automatic and semi-automatic cameras of this type. It also includes cameras which may have an interchangeable lens facility but have a top shutter speed of only 1/300th second or less.

ADVANTAGES
Quick and easy to use. Because the technical problems of exposure are

taken out of your hands with an automatic camera you may get shots which might otherwise have been missed while adjusting the camera.

LIMITATIONS	METHODS FOR GETTING THE BEST RESULTS
Slow top shutter speed. Non-interchangeable lens.	See Chapter Three for special techniques. Get as close to the subject as possible as a guide. On bright days when you can stop down the lens, do not try to shoot subjects more than 45 ft. from the camera. On dull days, when lens is working near full aperture, reduce maximum distance to 25 ft.
Limited maximum aperture on lens (i.e. anything less than f2).	Use fast film. If necessary, increase film speed by extra development time (see Chapter Five).
Lens quality not very high. Image definition poor at great enlargement.	Get in as close as possible. Use lens stopped down to f8 or f11 when this is possible. Position subject in view-finder so that the image is recorded on the centre of negative area where definition is at its best.
Viewfinder difficult to use when photographing fast-moving objects.	Fit frame finder.

Automatic cameras

LIMITATIONS	METHODS FOR GETTING THE BEST RESULTS
May under-expose subjects which have strong back lighting.	If fitted with setting lock, try to move in close (3 ft.) to take a reading, lock the setting and then go back to shooting position. If the camera has no setting lock, you can use a lower film speed on the setting dial than is actually being used in the

camera: i.e. *using* 400 ASA film, *set* 160 ASA. Only use this method with black and white pictures.

Range-finder cameras with interchangeable lenses and top shutter speed of 1/500th second or above (35 mm. format)
ADVANTAGES
Light, unobtrusive, silent in operation and easy to focus under low light levels. They are especially suitable for stage action shots.

LIMITATIONS	METHODS FOR GETTING THE BEST RESULTS
Not as easy to use with long lenses as an SLR.	Leica cameras may be fitted with reflex finder (Visoflex) for use with long lenses. A separate optical or frame finder may be an advantage with some cameras. See Chapter Six.
Electronic flash is synchronised at slow speed. Usually around 1/60th second.	

Single-lens reflex cameras with interchangeable lenses (35 mm. format)
ADVANTAGES
Quick and easy to use. Focusing and composition is simple even when using long lenses. Through-the-lens metering systems are very helpful with long lenses. Motor-drives can be fitted to leading designs of SLR's. These are very valuable in action photography. See Chapter Seven.

LIMITATIONS	METHODS FOR GETTING THE BEST RESULTS
Lenses (see Chapter Two for full explanation of problems). *Manual.* Screen gets dark as lens is stopped down. Hard to focus.	When the use of a manual lens is unavoidable, with very long focal length lenses it is sometimes impossible to design a satisfactory linkage between camera and aperture control – the only answer is to practise focusing techniques using the darker screen.
Pre-Set. You may forget to stop	Practise so that this becomes a

down lens just before taking the picture. reflex action akin to focusing. Buy fully automatic lenses if possible for action work.

Single-lens reflex cameras (6 cm. × 6 cm. or 6 cm. × 7 cm. format)
ADVANTAGES
The main advantage of using a large negative format is that you get top quality prints with fine definition. This is less important in action work than in, say, pictorial or industrial photography. For many, the bulk and high cost of this type of camera are detracting features.

LIMITATIONS

METHODS FOR GETTING THE BEST RESULTS

Top shutter speed of 1/500th second when fitted with Compur shutter.

See Chapter Three.

Synchronisation problems may occur with focal plane shutters which synchronise on electronic flash at around 1/60th second.

See Chapter Five.

Film backs may only take limited number of pictures – on 120 film, 12 frames usually – so you may run out of film at the crucial moment.

Plan your shots (see Chapter Four) and become proficient at rapidly changing film (see Chapter Three). Some large-format SLR magazines will take 220 film giving 24 exposures per loading, or may be bulk loaded with 5 m. (16·4 ft.) of 70 mm. film providing 70–80 exposures.

Twin-lens reflex cameras – fixed and interchangeable lenses
ADVANTAGES
Large negative format ensures good quality enlargements with high definition. On an expensive (£100-plus) TLR, the optical system should be good enough to allow small portions of the negative to be greatly enlarged. This helps overcome a few of the limitations imposed by the fixed focal length lens.

LIMITATIONS

METHODS FOR GETTING THE BEST RESULTS

Top shutter speed of 1/500th second.

See Chapter Four.
Fixed focal length lens.
Get in as close as possible. If the light is good enough to use a

Usually take 12 pictures on 120 film. You may run out at the critical moment.

slow emulsion, this will allow for maximum enlargement of a portion of the negative without obtrusive *grain* spoiling the definition.

Plan shots (see Chapter Four).

Interchangeable lens TLR's tend to be slower in use than SLR's.

Become skilled in fast re-loading (see Chapter Three).

Become very familiar with the operation of your camera (see Chapter Three).

Press cameras

Into this category come all large-format cameras – from 6 cm. × 7 cm. upwards – which have range-finder and/or ground-glass screen back focusing.

ADVANTAGES

Many second-hand cameras, such as the Speed Graphic and the MPP, can be acquired cheaply. Because they are sturdy cameras they will stand up to a lot of hard work. They can be used with ex-ministry lenses provided they have focal plane shutters. Many of the older models have both focal plane and Compur (between-the-lens) shutters.

LIMITATIONS

METHODS FOR GETTING THE BEST RESULTS

The focal length of even a standard lens will be such that the depth of field is more limited than on a miniature camera at each f-stop. This makes focusing harder.

See Chapters Three and Four for techniques which will improve your focusing. Get to know the camera well (see Chapter Three).

Maximum aperture of lens may be as low as f4.5 or f5.6. With long lenses f8 may be the maximum aperture.

Use fast film. Increase development times. You can do this with less fear of grain on a large negative (see Chapter Five).

Large-format cut film is costly.

Fit roll-film holder to take 120 film.

Limited number of pictures can be taken on roll film.

Plan shots (see Chapter Four).

Remaining camera types

Into this category come all large-format cameras—from 6 cm. × 7 cm. miniature Minox to 5 in. × 4 in. technical mono-rail cameras. However, none of these are really intended for action photography and they are so unsuitable that their limitations do not merit serious discussion here.

CHAPTER TWO

Lenses and Accessories for Action Photography

LENSES

Lenses for SLR's – aperture setting problems
Since with an SLR the image is viewed through the taking lens, consideration must be given to systems for stopping down the lens. Clearly it is going to be much more difficult to focus if you are looking at your subject through a lens which has been stopped down to f11 or f16. Where some long lenses are concerned this is unavoidable and focusing on a dim viewfinder screen is a technique which must be mastered. Many lenses, however, enable you to view the image at full aperture, and are only stopped down immediately prior to the picture being taken. There are two ways of doing this.

The simplest is the *pre-set lens*. In this system you adjust the aperture to the required f-stop but continue to compose and focus at full aperture. Just before you take your picture you twist a ring control which automatically stops down the lens to the pre-determined stop. After taking the picture it is necessary to twist the ring back again to view the subject at full aperture. These lenses are clearly easier to use than completely manual lenses, where you have to adjust the aperture to the required f-stop either by looking at the setting ring or by feeling for the click stops as you turn the aperture control. But pre-set or semi-automatic lenses, although cheaper to buy than fully automatic ones, have serious drawbacks when it comes to action photography. They are slower to use than automatic lenses and, more important, it is all too easy, in the excitement of the moment, to forget to twist the ring and stop down the lens. This means that the negative will be hopelessly over-exposed. Even if it is possible to correct such accidental over-exposure by drastic reduction in development time, the loss of definition and *depth of field* will probably result in a disappointingly unsharp picture. It is heart-breaking to lose a really dramatic action shot because you forgot to twist the aperture control. Those who have pre-set systems and have mastered them may well feel that I am being unfair to a method which is less expensive and which works well for them. You can certainly train yourself to use the pre-set lens so that stopping down before any shot is a reflex movement equal to focusing the lens. Even so, if you are starting out to build up a system of lenses with action work in mind, I strongly advise you to spend a little extra and get fully automatic lenses. These are triggered by the camera itself. As you press the shutter, a plate in the front of the camera body flips forward and stops down the lens to any pre-determined aperture. When the picture has been taken the plate moves back again and opens up the lens. This means you always focus and compose through a lens at full aperture, but you can never take a picture through an unstopped-down lens.

Wide angle lenses

Although such lenses may only be used now and then in action photography, do not overlook the possibility of capturing action shots which are 'different' by the imaginative use of a wide angle lens, especially in conjunction with a motor-drive camera. Such pictures often make very eye-catching and dramatic action studies, and their chances of finding an editorial buyer (see Chapter Nine) are greatly improved. Sports photographer Gerry Cranham, for example, mounted a motorised Nikon fitted with a wide angle lens behind a racetrack fence to record the moment when the horses came flying over. This picture provided a fresh look at a familiar subject and has been

PLATE 12
A standard lens provides an overall view of the 1964 Tokyo Olympic Games but the shot is lacking in impact

PLATE 13
A tele-lens, combined with panning technique (see Chapter Four), adds a feeling of speed and a sense of dramatic action to the still picture

widely publicised. I have fitted my own motorised Nikons to racing cars, aircraft and, in a waterproof case, to the front of a surf board. The most useful lenses for such work are the 28 mm. or 24 mm. focal lengths on 35 mm. (see also Part Two: Aviation and Sky-diving photography).

Standard lenses
In Part Two of this book I shall be looking at the specific equipment requirements and techniques needed to cover a wide variety of action subjects, from power boat racing to parachuting, from football to boxing. This list will show that the occasions when you need a standard lens for action work are few and far between. This is largely because, with the exception of special effects action shots using wide angle lenses, the need is always to get in as close as possible, and this involves the use of long lenses.

Long lenses
A 135 mm. lens on 35 mm. or a 150 mm. lens on a 6 cm. × 6 cm. camera is a useful general purpose long lens. It will enable you to get interesting studies over a wide range of subjects. But you will still need a much longer lens if you are to be in a position to cover all types of action. Long lenses bring the action to the photographer when it is either too difficult

or too dangerous to get in close with a camera. An assignment I shot for a magazine a couple of years ago illustrates one way in which these lenses can be, in this case literally, a life saver.

A girl artist decided that it would be interesting to paint on blown-up motor cars. The day she blew up her first 'masterpiece' I went along to record the action. The early sequences were easy – shots of her planting the explosives, under the watchful eye of a demolition expert, and an 'over-the-shoulder' shot of her about to blow up the car. But to get a picture of the moment of destruction I had to use a long lens and a radio control camera. I set up a motorised Nikon fitted with a 240 mm. Novoflex lens on a tripod some 80 ft. from the explosive-packed vehicle. Then we retreated to a safe distance and the car was blown. Dust, smoke and flying debris made all but one of the 36 frames shot by the camera useless ... but that one picture was enough to make the story a best seller. In the centre of the picture a large piece of debris can be seen hurtling towards the camera. This was a battered door which eventually ended up deeply buried in the mud right beside the camera – in *exactly* the spot where I would have stood if I had been operating the camera manually. If the equipment had been even a couple of feet closer, it would have been smashed (see pages 117–118).

To cover a wide range of action, from football to flying, lenses up to 400 mm. are useful. For some subjects you may need 1000 mm. lenses, but unless these are going to be used regularly it is just not worth tying up large sums of money in them. Far better to hire such monsters as and when the need arises. In Part Two of this book I have listed the types of lenses most suitable for covering a wide variety of action assignments.

Novoflex pistol mounts
In a conventional lens, focusing is achieved by means of a helical screw mount. By twisting the adjustment ring you move the front elements of the lens in and out. As focal lengths become longer and lenses heavier, such a method takes more and more time to operate. In the Novoflex system the lens is mounted at the end of a barrel consisting of two tubes, one tube sliding inside the other on ball-bearing rollers. A spring is mounted between the two tubes to keep them pushed apart, the maximum degree of separation being limited by metal stops. The tubes are pulled together by squeezing in a pistol-like grip. When the grip is fully depressed the lens is focused at infinity, when fully released it is adjusted to the closest focus possible with that focal length of lens. In operation the Novoflex grip is swift and positive, enabling the operator to change focus far more rapidly than would be possible with any other system. This is why so many Novoflex grips are used by sports photographers. Indeed, it would be hard to find any professional action

PLATE 14
The prying eyes of the
press! A magazine
photographer seeks the
protection of a car boot
while covering street
rioting with a 400 mm.
Novoflex lens and a
35 mm. (motorised
Nikon F) camera. Note
the pistol grip which is
squeezed in to focus,
and the supporting
chest/shoulder pod

photographer who does not have a Novoflex outfit amongst his most used equipment.

The system has been in use for many years and has seen a number of modifications and improvements. At present, the range of lenses for 35 mm. format consists of a 280 mm. f5.6, a 400 mm. f5.6 and a 600 mm. f8. All these lenses can be used with the same grip. Earlier versions had a screw thread mounting on the lenses but they have now been replaced by more positive bayonet-type mounts.

There are systems for 35 mm. and for 6 cm. × 6 cm. or 6 cm. × 7 cm. formats. For the larger cameras (Bronica, Hasselblad 1000F, Norita, Rittreck, and Pentacon 6, and the 6 cm. × 7 cm. format Pentax) there is a 500 mm. f5.6 lens. It may be useful at this point to explain the difference between a telephoto lens and a long focal length lens. In a telephoto construction a *negative* element is placed behind the normal *objective*. The effect is to produce the equivalent of a long focal length lens in a much shorter barrel. This compression makes for a more compact and less cumbersome lens. But the construction is more complicated and requires a very high degree of optical craftsmanship to ensure high definition. A long focal length lens is much simpler in construction without detriment to definition, but it does need a mount equivalent to the focal length of the element being used. This means that a 400 mm. Novoflex lens needs a barrel 400 mm. long. Thus the equipment is hefty and heavy. The fact that it also looks remarkably like a gun can cause the photographer some unexpected problems. There is an even greater risk of the lens being mistaken for an actual firearm when the Novoflex wooden rifle stock is used to help support it. I was once arrested in a Soviet Bloc country because local security officials mistook my lens, in its leather holster, for something rather nasty and lethal! In various trouble spots around the world, where the protruding snout of a 400 mm. Novoflex can look alarmingly like a bazooka, I know some photographers who have repainted the matt-black finish provided by

PLATES 15–17 (below and overleaf) When the unexpected happens a Novoflex enables the photographer to focus fast. Ed Lacey used a 400 mm. Novoflex lens on his motorised Nikon to take these award winning shots of a streaker who interrupted a rugby international

the manufacturers with a bright yellow gloss, simply to prevent trigger-happy soldiers firing first and asking questions later.

Novoflex lenses are not cheap, and you can only occasionally buy them second-hand. But if you intend to take up sports photography or any kind of action work seriously, you should try to find room in your budget for one. I suggest you buy the 280 mm. lens first and practise with that. The Novoflex system does take some getting used to, but once you have mastered it a whole new world of action picture possibilities will open up.

Zoom lenses

These allow you to change the focal length of the lens being used without removing it from the camera. Originally designed for movie cameras, and much used today by TV directors, the zoom lens has a

useful role to play in action photography – although, in my view, a less important one than the Novoflex. Given the choice between buying an expensive zoom or a Novoflex grip and two lenses, I would choose the latter every time.

Zooms can help you grab a picture which you might otherwise have missed, but like all sophisticated pieces of equipment they need to be handled correctly and used only in appropriate circumstances. There are three main reasons for using a zoom lens:

1 Because you may need to change very swiftly from a long focal length to a shorter focal length lens; for example, covering a race meeting, where you need to pull up individual cars as they round a bend and then grab a group shot of a bunch of cars jostling for position using a wider angle lens.

2 Where you need to frame your shot very accurately without

PLATE 18
A Nikon zoom lens fitted to a motorised Nikon camera. Focus is achieved by twisting the large ring control, zoom change by sliding it up and down. Swift change of focal length lens is, therefore, possible

PLATE 19 (opposite)
Long lenses take the photographer right in to where the action is ... but the price paid is limited depth of field, especially at wide apertures. This can be seen in this shot of Kenya's Kip Keino. 1000 mm. lens, shutter speed 1/1000th second f8

changing camera position. This only rarely happens in action work and is more valuable in pictorial photography.

3   To produce gimmick or special effect shots. Perhaps you have seen Gerry Cranham's pictures of 'blurred' action. He has used this technique on a wide range of subjects and produced some very effective action shots which have been widely used editorially and for advertising. The multiple-image effect is achieved by pulling in the zoom during the actual exposure.

Although they were first used in the cinema industry more than 40 years ago, the German firm of Busch produced an f2.8 zoom for the 16 mm. Siemens movie camera as long ago as 1930, it is only since the last war that work has been directed towards producing them for still cameras. There are considerable technical problems to be overcome, particularly loss of light and image quality due to internal flare from the many lens elements. Even today, many photographers would agree that the most expensive zoom lens is slightly inferior, at each of its focal lengths, to a fixed focal length equivalent. Some of the problems which the cheaper range of zoom lenses exhibit are:

1   Focus shift during zooming.
2   Loss of image contrast.
3   Various forms of distortion.

All these defects are inherent in any system which requires the very

accurate physical displacement of a number of lenses within the barrel of the zoom.

Medium-priced zooms may suffer from uneven definition, being better at some focal lengths than at others. They are also likely to exhibit pin-cushion distortion (the bending inwards of straight lines at the edge of the picture area) or barrel distortion (the opposite effect – the straight lines bow outwards). There may also be excessive flare when the lenses are used in very bright sunlight.

Of these faults, the most serious for the action photographer are focus shift during the zoom (readjusting the focus takes time and may cause a missed shot), flare and uneven definition. It is no good having a lens which will give you pin-sharp negatives at the 135 mm. focal length and fuzzy results at the 200 mm. focal length.

All except the highest-priced zoom lenses should be regarded as guilty of faults until proved innocent by being tested carefully before large sums are invested in them. For serious work, cheap zooms must remain a dubious proposition, although, given the rapid advances in optical design and lens-coating techniques, one should keep an open mind and base final judgement only on test results.

The controls on a zoom lens consist of focus change and focal length change – the ring which is used to zoom the lens in and out. On the more expensive zooms, such as the Nikon and Pentax, both these adjustments are made with a single control, a ring which has a combined twist and push-pull movement. On the Nikon zoom you focus by twisting the control ring and zoom in and out by sliding the ring up and down the barrel. With practice these two movements can be smoothly orchestrated so that the operation becomes fast and sure. Medium-priced zooms normally have separate controls for focus and zoom which makes them slightly slower in operation, but, even at its slowest, a zoom lens will always beat having to physically change lenses.

Perhaps the most hair-raising story of a zoom in action I know is told by a photographer on the London *Daily Mirror*. He was shooting a race meeting on a Nikon zoom with a range of focal lengths from 250 mm. to 85 mm. He was lying beside the track taking pictures as the cars came hurtling towards him. As the lead car approached he held it on 250 mm. It kept on coming and he slid down the focal lengths to hold it in his viewfinder . . . down and down he went . . . 180 mm. . . . 135 mm. . . . 85 mm. – by which time he suddenly realised that the lens was pointing upwards and the car was directly overhead. It had left the track and was 'flying' to destruction over the top of him. As he had been shooting with a motorised Nikon, at 4 frames per second, he captured the whole sequence and his pictures made a dramatic centre-page spread in his newspaper the following day. Without a zoom it is doubtful if he could have got that shot. It does show how the photographer, viewing the world in miniature through his viewfinder, may get so carried away that he forgets all sense of danger and may end up being literally carried away.

Ex-ministry lenses

These are mainly ex-RAF lenses used for aerial survey work. They often have enormous focal lengths (I once saw an 8 ft. monster!) and tend to be heavy and cumbersome. They almost all have to be tripod mounted. But for certain types of action (see Part Two) they can prove invaluable. Digging around second-hand shops you may come across an old newspaper or picture agency 'Long Tom' lens. These were designed mainly for cricket photography and have now largely been replaced by lighter, more compact and more flexible telephoto and mirror lenses. 'Long Tom' lenses had a focal length of 6 ft. or more and needed a small truck to cart them around. In fact, they were usually left in position, under cover of course, at the major cricket grounds. They can be used for certain types of action, but their weight and size make them impractical for general use.

Mirror lenses

A 400 mm. long focal length lens needs a barrel of the same length. Even using the telephoto principle to compress the physical length of the optical system, long lenses are still bulky. For example, a 300 mm.

PLATE 20
Some big lenses lined up to cover an athletics meeting. On the left is a mirror lens, on the right a more conventional long focal length lens. All are mounted on motorised cameras. Note the sturdy tripods used to provide really sure support.

telephoto lens is some 220 mm. long. Far greater compression can be obtained by using mirrors to 'fold' the light path and so reduce the length of the lens barrel.

In a mirror lens, light rays first pass through a refractive element which expands the image. This reaches a concave mirror which 'folds' the image back along its original path. Near their focus the light rays meet a second mirror placed just behind the first lens element. The light is then reflected a second time and passes back down the barrel and through a hole in the concave mirror where a further lens system collects and focuses it at the film plane.

Mirror lenses tend to be fat rather than long as the mirrors have a large diameter, and this makes them very hard to hand-hold. A further disadvantage is that the aperture is fixed. On 500 mm. mirror lenses the average aperture is f8, on 1000 mm. mirror lenses it is f11. This means that exposure has to be adjusted either using the shutter alone or in combination with different emulsion speeds and/or filters. Because the diameter of the mirror lens is so large it would be very expensive to fit filters in the normal way. To overcome this problem many designs allow filters to be fitted at the camera end of the lens. Other designs have a series of built-in filters changed by a control on the outside of the lens. To reduce the light without affecting it in any other way – for example, by using a yellow filter (which would be impossible with colour stock in the camera) – neutral density filters have to be used. These reduce the over-all amount of light reaching the film without selectively absorbing any part of the *visible spectrum.*

Cheap mirror lenses are often of dubious quality and should only be bought after testing. Second-hand mirror lenses should also be approached with caution because if they have suffered a hard knock the mirrors may have become displaced. Mirror alignment is very critical as any error is doubled up. Given the choice, I would always use a Novoflex system in preference to mirror lenses, despite the extra length.

ACCESSORIES FOR ACTION PHOTOGRAPHY
Tripods

My advice here is – get a good, sturdy one or don't bother. You will use the tripod to support long lenses and unless it does just that – really supports them – you are wasting your time and your money. I have seen some tripods being used which were about as steady on their feet as a drunk in the last throws of DT's. This is one item you can buy second-hand to cut costs. Do not think you must have something with lots of chrome and hundreds of movements. A sturdy wooden tripod, such as the Gandolphi, will give you all the support you need. Avoid tripods with ball and socket heads. The movement you will need most frequently is the side-to-side pan. If you buy a platform tripod – with a metal or wooden platform to hold the camera – you will have to add the pan head. Get a strong one with a smooth, easy side-to-side action and strong locking screws.

The occasions when you will need to use a tripod are limited. Of more value to the action photographer is a chest or shoulder support. The chest-pod consists of a short upright held by a harness around the photographers body. This can ease the burden of standing around keeping a long lens fixed on a subject. But make sure that the chest-pod, like the tripod, is strong enough to do the work required.

Light meters
Although many cameras are now fitted with a built-in meter, and most SLR's have some form of through-the-lens (TTL) metering, a separate light meter can be a useful accessory. If you have no built-in meter and intend to shoot reversal colour film (producing transparencies), then a meter is essential.

There are two types of meter. One works by measuring the resistance to an electric current in a cadium sulphide (cds) cell. The stronger the light falling on the cell, the less electrical resistance it has so the further the indicator needle deflects. Cds meters are fitted to most cameras which have a built-in metering system. Their advantage is that they are more sensitive under low light levels than the alternative selenium cell meter.

In the selenium cell meter, the cell produces a flow of electricity in proportion to the strength of light falling on it, so that the brighter the light, the more power is generated and the further the meter point deflects. The pointer of such a meter is held in position by a hairspring. To overcome the initial inertia of this spring a certain minimum flow of current has to be generated. With modern wide aperture lenses and emulsions it is often possible to take a picture under light levels which are too low to overcome this initial inertia and cause the selenium cell meter to register. The cds meter, with its power supplied by a tiny battery, is consequently more accurate in dim light. But when the cds meter's battery is exhausted the meter is useless, and that is one reason why I suggest that, if you have a cds meter fitted to your camera, you buy a reliable selenium cell meter – for example, a Weston – as a back up. It will enable you to check readings, and can be used if the cds battery should fail. More important, there are situations where you can get a more accurate reading using a separate meter than one built in to the camera. Having said this, it must be admitted that the modern TTL (through-the-lens) metering systems on high-priced SLR's are first class. They are especially valuable in action photography as they make the necessary corrections when using long lenses or filters.

Filters

There are only two filters of any value in black and white action photography. The first is an ultra-violet (u.v.) filter. This cuts down the haze encountered when shooting some subjects (i.e. aviation and sky-diving) but its main use is to protect sensitive lens surfaces from dirt, rain and sea spray. As the u.v. filter has no *filter factor* you do not need to make any changes in exposure when using one. Just screw it on to the front of the lens and forget it. I advise you to fit all lenses with a u.v. filter for protection.

The other type of filter which has the occasional value of enhancing the pictorial effect of certain types of action shot is the yellow filter. By absorbing 'blue' light it helps render clouds and makes skies look more dramatic. You can use it for sports meetings – for example, to make a more interesting study of a high-jumper silhouetted against the sky – or such subjects as sailing and boating, aviation and parachuting. In Part Two I shall indicate occasions when a yellow filter may usefully be employed. Remember that a yellow filter does have a factor (usually $\times 2$). This means that your exposure must be increased to make up for the light lost through absorption. For example, an exposure of 1/500th second at f11 without a filter becomes 1/500th second at f8 *with* a $\times 2$ yellow filter (see also Technical Glossary).

Lens hoods

These are essential, but there is no need to spend a fortune on them. I have found the cheap, screw-on, plastic hoods perfectly satisfactory. When buying hoods make sure that they are the correct length for the lens with which they will be used; too short and they can't do their job properly (their job largely being to prevent flare from the surface of the lens in bright sunlight), too long and they will tend to cut off the edge of the picture. This may not be noticeable at full aperture, but when the lens is stopped down the increased depth of field may be sufficient to cause the hood to mask out each corner of the negative. If in doubt, run a check on a short strip of film. But remember to stop the lens right down. If there is no cut-off at f22 then there won't be any at f2.

Carrying cases

These come in all shapes and sizes, from aluminium boxes to plastic bags. My own preference is for the aluminium container. These are slightly more expensive than thick plastic cases, although not any more costly than real leather gadget bags. If you can afford aluminium then I advise you to do so. After all, there is no point in spending several hundreds of pounds on a camera and lenses, then hauling them around in a flimsy container that cost less than a filter and gives the gear about as much protection as the average supermarket paper-bag. My philosophy has always been – carry the equipment around from job to job in a container which offers it maximum protection. Aluminium cases with rubber seals do just that. They can also be used for sitting on while waiting for something to happen and for standing on when something does and you need that little bit of extra height to photograph it.

Once I have arrived at the job, however, I transfer all the necessary gear out of the box and leave the container locked in the car or hotel room. I dislike carting gadget bags the size of small picnic hampers around on one shoulder. It is tiring and, more to the point, it gets in the way and slows you down if you have to move fast. When covering high-speed action subjects you may need to move very fast indeed – sometimes your life may depend on it!

So I set up my camera and then distribute the stray pieces of gear, films, light meter, lenses and so on, around the pockets of a very unfashionable but extremely useful jacket which I found in a sports goods shop. It was originally designed for hunting, shooting and fishing types and is waterproof, with dozens of pockets and pouches, all of which can be sealed with a button or a zip. For action work it is ideal. You can put spare lenses in the pouches, which are rubber lined for extra protection against the damp, and keep films in the zip-up pockets. I use one for unexposed colour film and one for unexposed black and white. All the exposed stock goes into yet another pouch. As a bonus, the jacket keeps me dry and warm.

Electronic flash equipment
The range of equipment available, its use and the types of flash most suitable for action photography will be discussed at length in Chapter Six.

In Part Two of this book, where I deal with 25 action subjects and discuss the specific techniques needed for the best coverage of each, I will indicate which types of camera are the most suitable.

But before you can use any camera, or any lens, successfully in the coverage of action subjects you must be completely familiar with the equipment. In the next chapter you will be able to discover how well you know your own camera and how you can get better acquainted.

CHAPTER THREE

The Key to Successful Action Photography

The pictorial photographer can carefully select his viewpoint and adjust his focus, the action photographer has to grab his pictures on the run – often literally. When the action starts there is usually no time to worry about exposures, viewpoints or precise focusing.

You snatch the pictures and may have no idea how good, or how bad, they are until the film has been processed. Sometimes a shot which didn't seem especially dramatic when you took it will turn out to be the best picture on the roll!

To shoot fast and successfully when the need arises you must be completely familiar with your camera. You must be its master, with an intimate knowledge of what it can and cannot be expected to do. Just as his instrument becomes part of the mind and body of a great musician, your camera must become an extension of your senses.

When they start to take pictures, many photographers possess this 'oneness' with their camera. They may begin by using simple equipment, possibly an automatic camera. They aren't worried about technique, aperture settings, or film speeds. To them the camera is an exciting new way of seeing and recording what they see. Many of their pictures are technically weak, but often they have captured rare moments of humour, beauty and drama. Then they become more proficient. They realise that their pictures aren't sharp enough, or are too grainy, or could be better exposed. The innocent enjoyment is replaced by anxiety about technique. The content of the picture becomes less important than how it is presented. Watch them at work. They stick the camera on a tripod, often quite unnecessarily except that it gives them a chance to fuss around. They move it a dozen times before they are satisfied, check the light reading every few seconds, put on and take off filters, change lenses, raise and lower the tripod legs. They worry desperately about grain size and print quality . . . now and then they may give some fleeting thought to what is on the negative. But only now and then.

It is a phase most photographers pass through, part of our education in photography. But such a cameraman is never going to make a great action photographer. By the time he is ready to shoot the parade will have long gone by.

Several years ago, soon after starting as a professional, I was sent by an agency to photograph a football match. I was just passing out of the 'anxiety about technique' stage, having spent two years at a photographic college. After checking the light a dozen times before the kick-off, I finally turned to the only other photographer near me at the goal mouth. 'What exposure are you giving it?' I asked. He was an elderly man with an antiquated press camera. He formed a circle with his thumb and one finger, then he held two fingers a short distance apart. 'About that by that. . .' he said. At first I thought he was merely trying to be funny at the expense of my inexperience. Not at all. He was showing me the relationship between the lens aperture and the slit on his roller-blind shutter. For me exposures were a matter of f-stops and shutter speeds. For this old-timer they were a question of making the iris diaphragm look the right size and setting the blind shutter to the right width for the job in hand. He never used a meter, but adjusted his equipment purely on the basis of experience and every shot was perfectly exposed. What is more, his pictures were pin-sharp, even though his camera had no range-finder and a long focal length lens which gave him only a limited depth of field.

He knew his equipment like an old friend. In anybody else's hands it might never have taken an acceptable picture; in his, as I later discovered, it produced consistently good results.

Before miniature cameras became commonplace in press photography, newspaper photographers worked with large-format cameras. These cameras imposed a number of limitations on their operators. For one thing, as I noted in the first chapter, their standard lens had a focal length at least double that of a 35 mm. standard lens. Because films were much slower than today, wide apertures had to be used frequently, especially for action photography demanding high shutter speeds. With a long focal length lens and a wide aperture, depth of field was often so slight as to be virtually non-existent. One footballer's face might be sharp, while the player standing directly behind him might be out of focus. There was no halfway-house; no stopping down to f16 and riding home on the back of depth of field. Many of the early cameras had no range-finders or other aids to focusing. The photographer estimated the distance, set it on the lens and relied on experience to get it right. Even today, some old Fleet Street men will talk of a picture being a 'two-yard shot. . .' or 'a one-yarder'. Furthermore, because they had to change dark slides after each picture, if they missed a shot it often stayed missed. Although an experienced press photographer could push in the sheath on his dark slide, extract the slide and replace it with a fresh one very swiftly, it was still painfully slow by comparison with today's thumb-swing wind on.

All these limitations forced the photographers to get their timing exactly right and focus their cameras perfectly the first time.

Today we tend to rely on very accurate range-finders or reflex screens to get our pictures sharp. Through-the-lens metering takes care of exposure problems. All of this is very helpful and convenient but it has tended to come between us and our cameras. Because they are so easy to use, we sometimes treat with indifference the mechanisms on which our pictures depend. Because they are so well designed and built, we take them for granted.

In some branches of photography you can get away with poor technique, thanks to depth of field, fast films, small f-stops, emulsion latitude and – in the last resort – the chance to reshoot.

Where action shots are concerned this is generally impossible. The picture is either in the camera or it never will be. Many action pictures are shot with long focal length lenses at wide apertures. So the face-saving depth of field vanishes. Focus must be accurate, often on fast and erratically moving objects. In order to get consistently good pictures our technique must be consistently good.

Perhaps it seems as though I am arguing against myself. Earlier I said that many photographers worried too much about technique and not enough about picture content. Now I am saying that for action shots, good technique is essential.

What this means is that the successful action photographer must combine the naïve spontaneity of the beginner with the technique of the experienced cameraman. Both qualities must be present in order to snatch shots and, at the same time, snatch them correctly.

A good analogy can be drawn between the action photographer and the skilled motorist. A learner driver has problems changing gear, using the clutch correctly and estimating distances when parking. With training and, above all, practice, these essential motoring skills become a reflex action. The proficient driver doesn't have to think about changing gear; his arm and leg perform the correct operations almost automatically. He doesn't worry whether there is room to pass or park; he can accurately estimate the distance.

This is the sort of proficiency which the action photographer must acquire. His picture-taking technique must become so automatic that it leaves him free to concentrate on the subject.

The first essential is to really know your camera. Perhaps you feel that you already have this knowledge. To find out, answer the following ten questions. Your answers must be quick as well as correct. If you hesitate and have to think about it then your camera is still too much of a stranger for high-speed action work.

Camera quiz

1 Your shutter speed is set at 1/30th second. You need to re-set it to 1/250th second. Do you turn the setting control clockwise or anti-clockwise when holding it in an operating position?

2 You have to change f-stops from f8 to f5.6. From the normal operating position, does the control turn clockwise or anti-clockwise?

3 On your standard lens (or the lens which you use most frequently) what is your depth of field at f8 when the camera is focused at

    a   10 ft;

    b   25 ft;

    c   infinity?

4 Look at an object between 6 and 12 ft. from you and estimate its distance. Now measure the distance. Were you correct to within 6 ins?

5 Repeat this test with an object over 25 ft. away from you. This time you should be accurate to within 1 ft.

6 Take out your camera and set the shutter speed to 1/60th second. Now, without looking at the camera, change the speed to the shutter speed directly below the top speed (i.e. if your top speed is 1/500th second then set it to 1/250th second).

7 Try loading a roll of film holding the camera in one hand. If you can manage this, do the same thing without looking at the camera.

8 Without looking at the camera, set the focusing scale to 6 ft.

9 Without looking at the camera set the aperture to f11.

10 If your camera has interchangeable lenses, try changing from one lens to another without looking at either camera or lens.

How did you do? If you found some of the tests difficult, don't worry. They will become second nature after only a little practice.

Why bother with them at all? You may feel that the occasion will never arise when you have to set the focus or aperture without being able to check your settings visually. This may well be true. But by practising all these skills, in the ways detailed below, you will become very familiar with your camera. If you are to be certain of capturing all types of action subjects and of never missing that perfect picture, then you must be able to use your camera instinctively. If you fuss and fret about focus and f-stops, lose time changing films or switching lenses, then you may pay a heavy price in lost shots.

For example, several years ago a press photographer was covering a political meeting in Japan. He was standing at the back of the hall, some 40 ft. from the platform. So far as he and his colleagues were concerned it was just a routine job. He had taken some close-up pictures of the speakers, using a 240 mm. Novoflex lens, and switched to a wide angle lens for a general view when he spotted a disturbance at the edge of the platform. Suddenly a youth armed with a sword stormed onto the stage and, before horrified officials could prevent it, had murdered one of the speakers. The whole incident was over in a few seconds. But in that time the press photographer changed back from wide angle to long focal length lens, focused and shot. His pictures of the assassination went around the world and won many awards. A less tragic example of having to act fast and instinctively happened to me on an assignment a couple of years ago. I was photographing a girl stunt cyclist attempting a record-breaking ride through a tunnel of fire. She broke the record all right and came hurtling out of the blazing straw tunnel just as it collapsed. I shot this on a 135 mm. lens. Then I moved in closer, thinking that the drama was over. But it had only just started! With a scream, the girl jumped from her bike, which had burst in to flames, and started to run across the field with smoke billowing from her pants. She was on fire. Her manager moved fast. He grabbed a bucket of water and hurled it over her, quenching the flames but making her yell all the louder. As I saw her leave the bike and run I knew that I was too close to capture the pictures on the 135 mm. lens. So I snatched a 24 mm. from my pocket, changed lenses, re-adjusted the f-stop for the correct exposure, raised and fired. If I had fumbled the lens change or the aperture setting then I would have missed the picture or produced over-exposed negatives.

PLATES 21–23 (right and opposite)
A girl stunt rider speeds out of a blazing straw tunnel. The camera was panned very slightly to convey speed without confusing the image of the flames and straw. 1/500th second f8 on a 135 mm. lens fitted to a motorised Nikon camera. When I had got this shot I thought the drama was over . . . but it had only just begun!

. . . with cries of alarm the girl jumped from her bike. The hot-pants had suddenly become very hot indeed. At this point I swopped to a 24 mm. wide angle lens and re-set the f-stop to get this shot. 1/500th second f11

. . . a bucket of water soon quenched the fire, if not the cries of alarm. 1/500th second f11

If you found any of the tests given above difficult – or impossible! – then I suggest you practise the exercises below. Try and do each of them once a day for about a fortnight. At the end of this time you will be amazed how much better you know your camera, and how much more confidence you have when handling it.

Exercise one
f-stop setting : An easy one, this, if your lens has click stops on the aperture ring, as do most modern camera lenses. You know how many f-stops the camera has. You know, or can easily check, whether a full turn to clockwise gives you the maximum or minimum f-stop. From this starting point it is possible to feel your way to any f-stop. Practise until you can set any f-stop without looking at the scale, and change from one f-stop in the middle of the scale to any other, again without making visual checks. If your lens is not fitted with click stops this 'blind' setting is still quite possible. But now you will have to judge the length of twist on the ring necessary to travel from one f-stop to the next.

Exercise two
Shutter setting : Now do the same exercise with your shutter speeds. Most shutter rings have a positive setting point for shutter speeds. Again, practise changing from one speed to another without looking at the settings.

Exercise three
Shutter/f-stop changes : You are shooting an athletics meeting. Your shutter/f-stop combination is 1/1000th second and f5.6. You need to take a line-up of runners leaving the starting line. You know that this can be captured at 1/250th second which will give you the smaller f-stop (f11) needed to obtain the necessary increase in depth of field. Practise changing both aperture and speed setting in this way. Think up different combinations and then see how swiftly and effortlessly you can make the two changes.

Exercise four
Exposure estimation : It is very useful to be able to judge exposures, not only in terms of initial f-stop/shutter speed combinations, but in changing light values. For example, suppose you are taking pictures at a football match. When you start it is bright and sunny, but clouds soon darken the sky. Can you judge how many f-stops you will need to open up to compensate for this? The worst conditions for changing light values are bright days with scattered, fast-moving clouds. It may not be possible to continually monitor the light, unless your camera has a built-

in (and preferably through-the-lens) metering system so an ability to assess these changing conditions accurately will be valuable. If you have a separate light meter, take it around with you for a few days. Practise estimating the light strength in relation to your maximum shutter speed. Learn to judge if it is 1/1000th second at f8 or 1/1000th second at f2 weather!

Exercise five
Distance estimation: It is important to be able to estimate distances correctly. Even with a range-finder or reflex camera it is still quicker to set a distance on the lens scale, raise and shoot. Sometimes it is only by swift response like this that you will capture an action shot.

To do this exercise you don't necessarily need a camera, as you can simply practise estimating the distances of objects between 10 ft. and 40 ft. from you. You can do this indoors, on the way to work, while out walking. Check your estimate by pacing out the distance as carefully as you can. Alternatively, you can use the range-finder or reflex focusing screen on your camera to check the distance. If you find your camera too heavy, or impractical to carry with you, but want to check distances accurately, then why not buy a pocket range-finder? You should practise this skill until you can estimate distances with an error of less than 10 per cent.

Distance estimation and hyperfocal distance: The hyperfocal distance of

PLATE 24
I was photographing an angler trying a new fishing aid – a floating armchair – when the unexpected happened. This shot was taken with a Hasselblad EL fitted with a 250 mm. lens. After this shot I put down the camera and started to load another magazine when . . . (see overleaf)

a lens is the distance from the lens to an object which is *acceptably* sharp when the lens is focused on infinity. It varies according to the aperture and the focal length of the lens being used. It can be very useful in action work as it enables you to *zone focus*. That is, instead of focusing on the object itself, which may be difficult if you are covering fast-moving action, you set the lens to the appropriate hyperfocal distance. Then everything between *half* that distance and infinity will be sharp. For example, if the hyperfocal distance of a lens is 16 ft. at f11, then by setting that lens to f11 and adjusting the focus to infinity everything from 8 ft. away from the camera and infinity will be sharp.

The hyperfocal distance can be worked out quite simply by using the depth of field marks on the lens barrel, or it can be taken from charts published in technical photobooks. You should note the hyperfocal distance of your most frequently used lenses and a range of stops, say f5.6, f8 and f11. When you have perfected the first part of this exercise, try estimating distances in relation to the various hyperfocal distances. For example, walking down the street you estimate a tree to be 20 ft.

away. Now take the hyperfocal length of a favourite lens at one of the f-stops. Suppose this is 30 ft. Walk towards the tree until you are at the edge of the hyperfocal distance zone of sharpness – in other words, at 15 ft. When you can do this easily with static objects, practise with objects moving towards you. Select a lens and f-stop, remember that everything from *half* the hyperfocal distance to infinity will be sharp. Now assess the moment when an object travelling towards you will pass out of 'focus'. This exercise is most valuable if you use it with the hyperfocal distances of long focal length lenses at wide f-stops. As I will explain in the next chapter, many action pictures will be more dramatic if the background is thrown out of focus; this can be achieved by limiting the depth of field through the use of wide apertures.

Exercise six
Shutter timing and distance estimation: The next step is to practise combining estimations of distance with the timing required to fire the shutter at the right moment. To do this you will need the help of a friend. Fit at least the standard lens on your camera. If you have a slightly long lens – for example, a 135 mm. focal length on 35 mm. format – this will give you harder but more useful training. Ask your friend to walk away from you and keep him or her in the camera viewfinder. At the distance where, leaving a small margin above and below the subject, he fills a vertical viewfinder on a full-length shot, note the distance. Now have him walk 10 or 15 yds. further on. Set the focusing scale to the distance which you found gave you a good-sized image in the viewfinder, and ask him to walk towards you. Watch him in the viewfinder, but do not alter the focusing scale. When he reaches the pre-determined distance, fire the shutter. There is, of course, no need to have the film in your camera for this exercise as you will be able to judge the accuracy with which you are carrying out the test by visual assessment. When you can capture movement at the pre-determined point every time, ask your friend to walk more quickly towards you, then to run towards you. When you can catch him at the right moment on every occasion, make the test harder by letting the camera hang around your waist until just before the critical moment. Then raise it swiftly, compose in a split-second and press the trigger. Incidentally, when firing the trigger during this exercise be very careful not to jab at the release button. This can cause blur, due to camera movement, even at speeds of 1/250th second. When you are confident of your ability with this test, put a roll of film in the camera and check your skill in a realistic situation. Go down to the local football ground and photograph amateur players. Note the distances at which the image of one, two or three will satisfactorily fill the screen. Now try taking shots of players running

towards you and at right-angles to your camera position. Incidentally, this skill is invaluable not just for action work but for candid photography too.

Exercise seven
Film loading : Even a 35 mm. camera giving 36 exposures can run out of film at a critical moment. With a 120 roll-film camera this is far more likely to happen. You must be able to change film quickly under adverse conditions. Get hold of a dud roll of film to practise with. First of all, rest the camera on a table or on your lap. Load and unload again and again until you can carry out the film change swiftly and effortlessly. Now make life harder for yourself by doing the operation standing up, holding the camera in one hand and film changing with the other. This is quite often necessary in action work where you may be standing on a muddy sports field or squatting in the back of a boat or aeroplane. When you can do it easily, try the same exercise wearing gloves. There may be occasions when you have to change films in bitterly cold conditions, either wearing gloves or when your numbed fingers will be equally insensitive and clumsy.

Two tips about film changing. Firstly, when unloading 35 mm. film, be careful to wind all the film back inside the cassette. When you are shooting fast it is all too easy to load an already exposed length of film into the camera. This, of course, ruins two sets of photographs and is, at best, very annoying! When you have wound all the film back inside the cassette you may get a little fogging through the felt light-trap, especially under very bright conditions. What I do is wind the film right back and then immediately put the cassette into its tin or plastic container.

The second point is make it a routine to always wind the film back fully before opening the camera back. If you forget you can fog valuable early exposures. If you have loaded the film with the 35 mm. leader or backing paper 'tongue' inserted very firmly into the take-up spool, the film may jam at the end. *Never* force the take-up mechanism. If it has jammed, and you are certain that all the film, except the leader strip on a 35 mm. film, which is designed to get fogged in any case, or the last few inches of backing paper on 120 or other roll films, has been wound back then open the camera. If in doubt, use a changing bag to check what has happened. Such bags are not very expensive to buy and can be invaluable for sorting out problems when working on location. I always carry a small changing bag around with me. If you have a 35 mm. camera and want to check whether or not there is a film in it, the technique is simple. Gently turn the re-wind handle without pressing the re-wind button or lever. You should immediately 'feel' the increased resistance on the handle. Even if you don't, the handle will rapidly lock if there is a film inside the camera, as the slack is taken up in the cassette. Never assume that a camera is empty. Always check before opening the back. Make this routine automatic and you will save yourself a lot of disappointment and expense at a later date.

Exercise eight
Lens changing : If your camera has interchangeable lenses, then it is important to be able to switch from one focal length to another without fumbling or delay. Screw threads pose many more problems than bayonet locks, which are quick and positive. When you are working swiftly it is all too easy to cross a thread and jam the lens. Today most interchangeable lenses and camera bodies are designed with bayonet mounts. Put one lens in your jacket pocket and have the second on the camera. Now, without looking at the camera, detach the lens, put it in another pocket and extract the second lens. Fit it quickly and without having to visually line up the bayonet locks. If you are unable to do this easily, practise by first making the connection while looking at what you are doing. When you can do this without difficulty put on a pair of gloves and repeat the exercise. Action photography is often a cold business and the ability to work with gloves on is a useful – and comforting – skill.

These eight basic exercises will provide you with a sound camera handling skill for action photography. They will also improve your general picture-taking technique. Make a close friend of your camera. Know how it feels and sounds in action. Play with it, learn to make focus and aperture adjustments without having to check the figures on the setting scales. Only by acquiring such intimate awareness of your camera can you combine good technique with instinctive shooting ability.

Summary
1   Photographers with no technical knowledge often shoot technically poor pictures which have a refreshing immediacy.
2   A self-conscious awareness of technique can lead to technical merit becoming more important than the actual content of the picture.
3   For action photography *sound technique* must be combined with the ability to raise and fire the camera swiftly.
4   Acquire this instinctive picture-taking ability by getting to know your camera intimately and by practising the basic skills.

CHAPTER FOUR

Visual Anticipation and Timing

Because there is usually no chance to do anything except fire the shutter once a piece of action has started, all the necessary preparation must take place beforehand. Often this means no more than spending 10 minutes selecting the best viewpoint, checking exposures and doing any pre-focusing which is possible. Sometimes hours or days of preparation go into a single action picture. I once spent a week organising a sequence which took exactly 10 seconds to shoot.

This visual anticipation is one half of the formula for success in action photography; the second half is timing. In this chapter I want to discuss both these essential techniques.

VISUAL ANTICIPATION

An action picture can be divided into three elements:

1 The action itself – this may be a man sprinting, an aircraft crashing or a racing car screaming around a tight corner.

2 The technique used for capturing this action – this includes camera angle, lens, shutter speed and any movement of the camera or lens to produce a special effect.

3 The background against which the action takes place.

These three elements must be considered in some detail, as they form the essential components of *visual anticipation*.

Action

Movement may be divided into one of three types.

Type One: Side-to-side action – for example, cars racing, horses galloping, men sprinting.

Type Two: Up-and-down action – for example, rugger players leaping for a ball, basket-ball players jumping for the net.

Type Three: Action which is a combination of both types – for example, a footballer while heading a ball may also be moving forwards or sideways.

PLATE 26 (opposite) Typical side-to-side action, an athlete breasting the tape shot on an Erniman $2\frac{1}{4} \times 3\frac{1}{4}$ in. press camera fitted with a roll-film back.

In placing action in these categories we are not concerned with the *position* of the camera in relation to the action. For example, racing cars may be photographed from the front or from behind, but the action remains, for the purposes of this classification, side-to-side action, in that its main direction is left-to-right or right-to-left. Similarly, you

PLATE 27
Up-and-down action as professional footballers leap for a high ball.

PLATE 28 (opposite)
A combination of side-to-side and up-and-down action during netball.

may photograph up-and-down action from above, or even below, but it remains in the second category because its main direction is firstly in defiance of gravity, then in response to it.

Technique

This preliminary analysis of action is important because it affects the way in which the movement can, or must, be photographed. There are seven factors to be considered when photographing any type of action.

a Speed and direction of the moving object.
b Speed of the shutter.
c Distance between the subject and the camera.
d Angle between the subject and the camera.
e The light.
f The f-stop and focal length of lens being used.
g Techniques for deliberate blur of subject or background.

Let us take them in turn and see how each factor must be related to our classification of action into three types.

Speed and direction of moving object. Let us suppose that we want to freeze some split-second of action so that the moving object is pin-sharp (as we shall see later, this is not always either possible or desirable). If the object is travelling at right-angles to the camera (Type One Action), then whether or not we can freeze it will depend on two variables. The first is the speed of the object, and the second is the speed of the shutter which we can use.

For example, a shutter speed of 1/60th second would be fast enough to freeze a person walking across the path of the camera. But if the person started to run, it would need a 1/250th or a 1/500th second to freeze the image. A sports car travelling at 80 mph would be blurred even at 1/500th second and quite probably at 1/1000th second. The first rule of action photography is simple and straightforward. Providing that the distance between the camera and the subject *does not increase*, then the faster the movement at 90° to the camera lens, the faster the shutter speed necessary to freeze it.

I emphasise the words *does not increase* because the distance between the camera and the subject has an important bearing on the speed needed to freeze movement. The closer the subject the faster the shutter speed which will be required. If you look out of the window of a moving train, telephone poles close to the track whisk past in a blur, while trees or posts at a distance seem to move much more slowly.

The relationship between shutter speed and subject distance can be expressed by this simple rule: each time the distance from the subject to the camera doubles, you can halve the speed of the shutter needed to freeze it; each time the distance halves, you must double the shutter speed required. For example, a shutter speed of 1/500th second is found to be sufficient to freeze a sprinter at a distance of 20 ft. from the camera. If you move in to 10 ft., then you must double the shutter speed to 1/1000th second to stop movement in the same way.

What happens when you stay at the same distance from the moving subject but change to a longer focal length lens? You will still need to increase your shutter speed. The acceptance angle of the long focal length lens is much narrower than the standard lens, therefore the object will pass in and out of its field of vision more rapidly.

In practice it is necessary to get in as close as possible to your subject, so this factor cannot effectively be used for shooting action at slower shutter speeds, either because of camera limitations or light problems. As I mentioned in Chapter One, blowing up a small portion of a negative is not really satisfactory, especially when that negative has been shot with an inexpensive lens. Of far more use to photographers who have to shoot action at fairly slow shutter speeds is the fourth factor in our list.

PLATE 29
An almost head-on camera position has enabled the photographer to 'stop' these high speed racing cars at 1/250th second. But the picture is lacking a sense of action.

Angle between the subject and the camera. To freeze an object travelling at right-angles to the camera requires a shutter speed in relation to the speed of movement. The faster the movement, the higher the shutter speeds. An object travelling, even at high speed, towards or away from the camera can be successfully photographed at fairly slow shutter speeds.

Some books on photography have movement analysis charts which give approximate shutter speeds for subjects travelling at different speeds and at varying distances from and angles to the camera. I think such figures are unnecessary. If when you are confronted by an action subject you are going to try and remember a chart, your camera-work will be a very hit-and-miss affair. Of far greater importance than specific shutter speeds are the two simply remembered general rules:

1 The closer the subject, the faster the shutter speed needed to freeze both subject and background.

2 The nearer that the angle between subject and camera approaches 90°, the faster the shutter speed needed to freeze both subject and background.

The next two factors, light and f-stop, interact in a way which will be familiar to all photographers. But in action work one of the variables in the shutter speed/f-stop combination, the shutter speed, is often dictated by the type of action and the distance and angle at which the subject is photographed. Under these circumstances the f-stop must, of course, be adjusted to fit in with the shutter speed and film speed. Because of focusing problems and the limited depth of field available when using long lenses at wide aperture, it may be necessary to increase the film speed in order to use a satisfactorily small f-stop. I will discuss these techniques fully in the next chapter.

The seventh and final factor on our list is the use of blur, either in the subject or, more usually, in the background.

So far we have talked about the problems and techniques for freezing action. But not every action subject should be transfixed like a butterfly on a mounting-board. If you shoot a racing car so that it looks as though it is stationary, then it would have been easier to photograph it that way. Furthermore, if the background is sharply focused and obtrusive, it is going to distract the viewer from the main part and point of the picture. This will reduce the drama and impact of your photograph.

The technique for blurring a background is termed *panning*. Panning means following a moving object with the camera and pressing the shutter while the camera is still travelling. This has the effect, shown in picture 11, of blurring the background while keeping the moving object sharp. It enables moving objects to be shot at fairly slow shutter speeds. The motorcyclist in the photograph was captured at a speed of 1/60th second, even though he was moving at about 70 mph. This is clearly

PLATE 31
At 90° to the camera panning will be necessary – and desirable – to freeze a very high speed object even at top shutter speeds. Here a speed of 1/1000th second has been used with panning to produce a sharp picture full of a sense of speed and drama

going to be important to photographers with slow top shutter speeds on their cameras. But panning should not merely be regarded as a device for taking action pictures at slow shutter speeds. Its main function is to convey a feeling of movement in a still picture, which is one of the major difficulties facing the action photographer.

When should you blur and when should you try and get everything sharp? The answer depends on two things. First, and of overriding importance, is the effect you want to achieve. If your intention is to get action pictures in which everything is deliberately blurred – for example, to provide an eye-catching colour shot – then this is the main consideration. But under all other circumstances the answer depends on which type of action you are shooting.

PLATE 32
A head-on shot can be dramatic provided the side-to-side action is accompanied by up-and-down action. When gravity is defied there is an immediate feeling of speed and movement

Type One (side-to-side). As a general rule the subject should be sharp, but it is very useful to blur the background by panning in order to convey a sense of speed and movement.

Type Two (up-and-down). If an object is defying gravity, then this fact alone will convey a sense of movement. We know that the footballer leaping after a high ball is going to tumble back to earth. The impact of the shot comes mainly from showing the eye what it would never otherwise be able to see, a split-second movement frozen for ever. A

general rule for Type Two action, therefore, is to keep it all as sharp as possible. This does not necessarily mean using a very high shutter speed. Up-and-down activity can be divided into three stages. The object goes up, it stops for a moment at the peak of the movement, then it comes down. In its going up and its coming down, the subject may be travelling so fast that it needs a high shutter speed to freeze the movement. But if you catch it at its peak, then there is no actual movement of the main part of the subject. You can therefore freeze it at a fairly slow speed. What is more, because this moment of inertia at the peak of the upward movement represents the ultimate second of supreme effort, by capturing it you will get a far more effective shot. For example, a basket-ball player jumps high towards the net. If you caught him during the upward or downward movement, a speed of 1/1000th second might be insufficient to freeze the moment. But he uses up his momentum and comes to rest; for a split-second, his body is stationary. His face will be set in a grimace of desperate determination, every muscle exerting its maximum effort to reach the desired goal. At 1/250th second you may get his face and body pin-sharp, the extremities of the arms and legs, perhaps moving sideways, may be slightly blurred. But this will only add to the drama and sense of movement.

PLATE 33
A combination of Type One and Two action can pose the greatest problems for the photographer. To pan or not to pan. The rule is this: if the action is mainly Type One (side-to-side) pan; if it is mainly Type Two (up-and-down) use a high shutter speed and an angle at which you can freeze everything. This is mainly, and most importantly, Type Two action.

Type Three (combination of Types One and Two). This can present the greatest problems to the photographer. To blur or not to blur? If the essential part of the picture consists of Type One action, then consider blurring the background. If it is mainly Type Two, use a high shutter speed to get the subject sharp and freeze movement. Usually common-sense will dictate the best course of action. For example, picture 33 is mainly side-to-side action, the car is travelling out of the van. But any attempt at panning would have blurred the furniture van and made it much less clear what was happening. In Section Two of this book I shall provide notes about the type of action involved and the techniques which can be best used.

Conveying action in a still photograph

I have already discussed the technique of panning for putting movement into Type One action shots. There are four other ways of suggesting movement on a still photograph.

1 *Composition.* During the storming of the Japanese-held Iwo Jima during the Second World War, a combat cameraman caught the moment as the American flag was raised over the island. His photograph showed a group of GI's looking at the vertical flag pole up which the

PLATE 34
Poor composition, bad editing and confusing foreground and background have turned a potentially dramatic action picture into a dull shot. Try cropping this picture with L-shaped sections of card to see how it might be improved

stars and stripes was being raised. It was a dramatic moment but the picture has little drama. A few days later another picture was taken – a group of soldiers struggling to raise an angled flag pole. The picture was so dramatic, so full of atmosphere and action, that it became world famous. This illustrates the basic point about action picture composition.

Horizontal and vertical lines are static and restful.
Diagonal lines suggest movement and drama.
Balance in a composition is dull.
Imbalance, provided it is not overdone, suggests motion and unrest. Picture 34 shows the moment when a stunt driver hurled his car into the side of a coach. It sounds dramatic. It looks deathly dull.

This picture could be improved, as could many action pictures which don't quite seem to have made it, by cropping. There is too much distracting muddle in the foreground and too much background for the eye to concentrate on the subject. You can see the difference which this would make by masking the picture with a sheet of card top and bottom. Try the same technique on your own action shots. If you cut two L-shaped masks from black card you will have a very effective editing tool.

PLATES 35–37 (below and overleaf) Judo kids sequence shows how a series of pictures will help convey action. Note how contrasting background and backlighting have been used to give this sequence maximum impact. A confusing background would have detracted greatly from the photographs.

2 *Sequence shooting.* The second method for suggesting action in a still photograph is to take a sequence of shots so that the viewer can follow a piece of action through from start to finish. This is simple film-making using a still camera and it can be very effective. I am often amazed that so few photographers attempt sequence work. Perhaps they feel that if they catch one moment of action, that is the best they can hope for. A motorised camera is very useful, though by no means essential, for this work. The marvellous judo kids sequence was taken on a manual wind camera, for example. Motorised sequences will be found in Chapter Seven.

3 *Expressions.* Facial expressions and body positions can convey action and movement very powerfully. Getting the best expressions is largely a matter of timing and this will be dealt with in a moment.

4 *Flying material.* Mud flying from the hooves of racehorses, or spinning up beneath the wheels of an autocross car, wood splintering as a racing car smashes through a boundary fence, spray leaping into the air behind a speed boat – all this secondary movement helps to convey a feeling of high-speed action. There is no need to use a high shutter speed to freeze it; very often a slight blur improves the sense of movement.

PLATE 38 (opposite)
Facial expressions can
help to convey move-
ment and drama. Myra
Nimmo of Scotland
during the long jump at
the Xth Commonwealth
Games in New Zealand
in 1974

PLATE 39
Flying mud, spray or
debris can convey a
sense of movement in a
still picture, and make
the shot more eye-
catchingly dramatic

Backgrounds

This is the third component of VAT. I have already discussed one way in which backgrounds can be rendered unobtrusive, by blurring through panning techniques. But where blurring is impossible it is important that the background does not distract from the main subject. When this happens the picture, however powerful the moment of action which has been captured, will lack drama.

Backgrounds distract the viewer when they are:

a Of equal sharpness to the foreground subject.

b Very close in tone to the foreground subject.

The problem of focus similarity is reduced in action photography because so many pictures are taken at fairly wide apertures on long focal length lenses and thus the depth of field is too limited to bring both subject and background into sharp focus. When using a wide angle or standard lens it is essential that you work as close to the subject as possible and use a wide f-stop, unless the subject itself demands great depth of field. If you are able to determine the positioning of the subject in relation to the background, then move the subject as far away as possible to ensure that the background is out of focus.

The difficulties which arise when foreground and background are similar in tone are less easily overcome in action photography, where the photographer usually has very little control over his subject. The only thing to do is to try and select a viewpoint which provides the maximum contrast. Low angles often do this by throwing the subject against the sky. When looking through the illustrations in this book, pay special attention to the ways in which the backgrounds have been handled, and notice how an obtrusive background reduces the impact of the photograph.

TIMING

Although correct timing of the shutter release is extremely important in action photography, there is not a great deal which can usefully be written about it, as the only way to achieve a sense of timing is by practice.

There is a tendency, especially amongst beginners in action photography, to press the shutter release too soon rather than too late. This can produce a less dramatic and interesting picture, as the photographs of the car jumping over blazing straw illustrate. A split-second's delay in firing the shutter has made all the difference. The main reasons why the second picture has more impact than the first is that the car is closer and that the diagonal line of composition is much stronger (Pictures 42 and 43).

PLATE 40 (top left) If this background had been other than strictly neutral and offering a stark tonal contrast to the subject the picture would have been very confusing and the vital ball probably invisible.

PLATE 41 (bottom left) A confusing background distracts attention and detracts from the action. Even cropping will not help this shot much because the main subject and the background are so close in focus and tone.

VISUAL ANTICIPATION AND TIMING IN ACTION

Now that I have outlined the elements of VAT in theory, let us look at them in practice. Let us look at two typical action subjects to see how they can be put into practice.

Assignment One : Stock Car Meeting
Weather conditions : Overcast afternoon sky in winter. Meter suggests exposure of 1/1000th second at f5.6 rating the film at 800 ASA.
Equipment : 35 mm. SLR with 240 mm. Novoflex lens, 135 mm. telephoto and 35 mm. wide angle lens.
Visual anticipation : From previous experience at the track, I know that most of the spills occur on two corners. A track pass enables me to stand in the centre of the arena, but as cars tend to bounce off the track on to this area, a close watch must be kept at all times. The organisers make it clear I am in the position 'at my own risk'. Before the race I line up some possible angles. From the centre of the arena, with a 240 mm. lens, I will be able to obtain panning shots of cars, from the edge of the track, 45° shots of cars approaching me with a 135 mm. lens.

PLATE 43
A split second later and
the shot becomes
dramatic

Technical considerations arising: 1/500th second will be sufficient for 45° shots, and 1/250th second adequate to freeze movement on panning shots. However, on one bend serious spills are likely. Such crashes will be a combination of up-and-down and side-to-side action, so it will be essential to use a 1/1000th second in order to freeze everything.

Decisions: Select viewpoint where bends and dangerous corner can be covered. Get shots of cars approaching at f8 or f11 which allows plenty of depth of field. As cars bunch on dangerous corner, go swiftly to 1/1000th second at f5.6 in case of accidents.

Assignment Two: Athletics Meeting
Weather conditions: Dull. Meter gives an exposure of 1/500th second f2 at 400 ASA. Decide to push film speed so that I can get 1/1000th second f5.6.
Equipment: 35 mm. SLR with 135 mm. lens, and 28 mm. wide angle lens.
Visual anticipation: I go around to each part of the track. I decide to photograph the high jump from a low angle and check the possible

camera positions. From one of them the low angle, coupled with the depth of field of the 28 mm. lens necessary to get this shot, will mean that floodlights in the background are obtrusive. I select a viewpoint from which the background will be sky, and ask an official to keep the spot for me.

I decide to photograph the hurdles from front on. If a side view is taken, then panning will be necessary at 1/500th second. This will blur the hurdles and make the picture confusing. So I settle for front on, with the 135 mm. lens to compress the perspective. Before race starts I pre-focus and shoot picture as leaders reach the pre-determined spot.

These, then, are some of the technical and visual considerations which you might apply. Visual anticipation means working things out before the action starts so that you eliminate as many difficulties as possible. Timing means learning to press the release button at the critical moment. Both must be learned by practice.

Shooting action with simple cameras
1   When you have a limited top shutter speed, shoot side-to-side (Type One) action by:
a   Panning.
b   Taking the shot front on, or at 45° to the subject. Avoid fast movement at 90° to the camera.
2   Take up-and-down movement (Type Two) by timing your shots to coincide with the peak of action.
3   Where action involves both types of movement (i.e. football matches), try and select moments where mainly Type One or Type Two action is taking place. Then use the techniques given above. For example, if covering rugger, you may be able to capture a line-out by timing, or a sprint towards the touch-line by panning. But a movement which combines Types One and Two, such as the ball being flung clear of a scrum, is not likely to be sharp enough at slow shutter speeds.

Summary
1   Plan your action shooting in advance.
2   Use special techniques to give your pictures a feeling of movement.
3   Compose on a diagonal line whenever possible.
4   Get in close at the shooting stage if possible; if not crop carefully at the printing stage.
5   Unnecessary background and foreground distracts and reduces the drama of an action shot.
6   Try and throw the background out of focus by use of depth of field.
7   Try and obtain a tonal contrast between subject and background.

CHAPTER FIVE

Films and Processing Techniques for Action Photography

BLACK AND WHITE FILMS

Despite the value of panning and slow speed techniques, the majority of action shots are still taken at shutter speeds of between 1/500th and 1/2000th second. Working in a dull light, with a long lens stopped down to f8 or f11 in order to produce adequate depth of field, will demand a fast film; for example, Kodak Tri-X stock which normally is rated at 400 ASA.

There will be many occasions when this recommended speed is not high enough and the film will have to be rated at 800 ASA or higher in order to get a printable negative. To achieve this increase in speed, the development time must be extended. But 'pushing' the emulsion in this way produces two side effects:

a An increase in contrast.
b An increase in grain size.

If necessary, slight increases in negative contrast can be compensated at the printing stage (by using a soft grade of bromide paper) but a slightly contrasty action shot is not unattractive. If the picture has been taken on a dull day, this increase in contrast will be extremely useful. Furthermore, given two identically sharp pictures, one printed soft and the other slightly hard, people will usually say that the more contrasty photograph *looks* sharper.

The increased grain size is less desirable as it reduces definition. However, as an action shot can get away with being more contrasty than, say, a landscape or portrait picture, so you can get away with rather more grain than in other types of photography, provided the subject is dramatic and eye-catching.

Although there is no way round the increase in grain size when pushing development times, you can minimise the effects of extra development by taking care to balance solution temperatures during processing. A rapid change in temperature, say between the developer and the fixer, or the fixer and the wash, can cause clumping of the silver halide particles which leads to an increase in grain size.

Processing techniques for minimum grain on forced development
1 *Preliminary wash.* Some photographers like to rinse the film in

PLATES 44–45 (above and opposite) Contrast can make an apparent difference to image sharpness. These two shots are equally sharp on the negative, but the soft, 'muddy' print (Plate 45) looks less sharp than the more contrasty picture

clean water before starting development. The theory is that this slightly softens the emulsion and prepares it for the developer. Others go straight to the development stage. When you use a pre-dev. wash, make sure that the water is within ±1° of the development temperature. Use an *accurate* thermometer, not a cheap one and unreliable one.

2 *Development.* You can force the development of a film in two ways: by increasing the temperature or by increasing the processing time. The most satisfactory method is to increase both. Develop at around 70°F instead of 68°F and leave the film in the developer for an extended period. Just how long you should develop the film depends on the make of film and the developer being used. Below you will find a list of film/developer combinations which are most suitable for increasing film speeds. As a general guide, film rated at 400 ASA may be uprated to 800 ASA merely by increasing the developing temperature to 70°F and keeping the processing time the same as for standard development. By combining 70°F with a 50 per cent increase in processing time, the film speed will be increased to 1600 ASA. By combining the higher temperature with 100 per cent increased time the film can be pushed to 3200 ASA. These figures are a *guide* only, and assume that processing is taking place in a 'normal' film developer (i.e.

D76) as opposed to a developer designed to give extra speed (i.e. Acuspeed).

3 *Stop-bath.* The temperature of this solution must be within $\pm 1°F$ of the developer.

4 *Fixers :* Again, keep the temperature within the $\pm 1°F$ range of the other solutions.

5 *Final wash :* The first few minutes of the final wash must be held within the $\pm 1°F$ range of the other solutions. To plunge the film into a bucket of tap water after taking care of the temperatures during the early processing stages is to undo all your good work, and it will be especially damaging if you have increased the development temperature. Unless you have a thermostatic mixer control on the wash water supply, the easiest way is to fill a bucket with water at the correct temperature. Fill the tank, agitate and throw away the water. Re-fill and agitate again. Do this a few times, and then add a little cold water to the wash bucket to slowly bring down the temperature to that of the tap. Once you have reached this temperature you can complete the wash under the tap in the usual way.

When to 'push' films
The simple answer is usually when you have got no other choice. It is

always best to work at the manufacturer's stated speed where possible. However, films do have a certain amount of latitude. For example, a film normally rated at 400 ASA could be exposed at 650 ASA and still developed normally to yield an acceptable negative.

Some subjects will stand increased development better than others; for example, football matches where the contrast range is usually limited – unless one team is playing all in white. Cricket matches, on the other hand, with their high contrast and large areas of white, are difficult subjects to print from contrasty negatives.

Increased development for contrast

Suppose you have a subject of low contrast photographed on an overcast day when the light is bright but very flat. Under these conditions you may well get a better print by increasing the development to push up the contrast. In order not to make the negative too dense, under-expose the film in the camera. For example, your meter reading gives you an exposure of 1/1000th second at f8 with the film exposed normally at the manufacturer's recommended speed. So you deliberately expose at, say, f11. Then you can increase the development time to give you that extra bit of bite in the contrast,

PLATE 46
Subjects with large areas of light tone, such as water sports, must be carefully processed. If the contrast is increased too much by extra development then there will be insufficient detail in the vital high-light areas. A filter can be useful for increasing contrast between sky and water or sky and clouds. Russian MTO 500 Mirrorflex lens on Nikon F 1/1000th second f9

without having a negative which is too dark. Some action photographers use this technique all the time, rating 400 ASA film at 650 ASA so as to get extra contrast in all their negatives.

FF/DD technique

This is a technique for increasing the film speed only on *certain frames*, a remarkable advantage the FF/DD has over all other processing methods. In one test a darkroom technician processed a roll of 36-exposure 35 mm. Tri-X film which had been exposed at speed ratings ranging from 200 to 3000 ASA. All the negatives were printable! This method clearly offers a tremendous saving to the occasional film user. If you have some important pictures on your roll of film, shot at the normal rating, and then have to uprate the same length of film drastically to cope with action under poor light, you can do so – without sacrificing the early frames.

I have only used FF/DD with a combination of Tri-X and D76 developer.

Processing. Dilute concentrate D76 8 times. Agitate the film continuously, but not over vigorously for two minutes. Then leave it

PLATE 47

A dull day, so uprate the film and increase development to improve contrast. Here the light reading suggested an exposure of 1/1000th second f8 at 400 ASA. But in order to increase contrast film was rated at 650 ASA and exposure made at f11. Film was developed in D-76 for 14 minutes at 68°F

alone for the remainder of the processing time, which will be from 40 minutes to one hour. The development temperature is 68°F and this must be stringently maintained in all the solutions, including the final wash.

The theory is that the developer soon exhausts itself in the highlight areas but carries on working in the shadows, building up the required density. There is no increase in fogging, nor in contrast. A wedding photographer I know uses FF/DD on all his white weddings and uprates his Tri-X to 1600 ASA with no subsequent printing problems.

Experiment with FF/DD before you use it on an important roll of film. A clinically clean approach to processing is essential. All tanks, measuring beakers and containers must be carefully washed before use. Discard developer after use. Using FF/DD, speeds up to 4000 ASA can be achieved.

Film/Developer combinations for action
Kodak Material
Tri-X Film/D76. Use at 68°F, diluted 1+1 and throw away the developer after use. When pushing up the speed, keep agitation gentle. A 50 per cent increase in development time (about 20 minutes with Tri-X) will produce an ASA speed of around 1600.

Tri-X Film/Microdol-X. Process at 70°F with an increase of 50 per cent in time for an uprate to 1600 ASA. Grain tends to be slightly finer than with D76. This is a clean working developer which does not lead to chemical fogging even in forced development.

Tri-X Film/HC110. A fast-working developer from Kodak which gives moderately fine grain, maximum shadow detail and a long density scale without loss of film speed or sharpness. HC110 has wide development latitude and a low fog level on forced development. Can be diluted from 1+15 to 1+79 times.

Tri-X+Acuspeed. Gives very good sharpness at speeds up to 1600 ASA. Take great care during processing as staining can result from messy development technique. Use a stop-bath between developer and fixer.

Tri-X+Diafine. Diafine is a two-bath developer and all films get the same processing time – 3 minutes in each bath. Time remains constant at any developing temperature within the recommended range. This makes it very easy to use. Care must be taken not to contaminate Bath A with Bath B. This developer has an almost indefinite shelf-life; you can put it away and come back to it months later. Speeds up to 3200 ASA are possible (see also HP4 below).

Tri-X+Promicrol. A dilution of 1+3 and a development time of 15 minutes at 68°F will give a speed of 800 ASA. Extra development

PLATE 48 (opposite) Increasing development times push up contrast and grain. But grain is less important on action shots than in other types of photography. Sometimes it can add to the overall impact.
  Circus shot on Pentax camera. 1/250th second f2.8. Film rated at 1600 ASA.

yields speeds up to 3200 ASA without much risk, and gives a fairly fine grain result. This combination does need care in handling to produce clean negatives.

2475 Recording Estar+DK50. Probably the fastest combination in the world. 2475 Recording Estar was designed for low-light surveillance work by bodies such as the FBI. It is a very grainy emulsion only suitable for special effects or for use when no other stock will produce the required results. The basic film speed is 1600 ASA and it can be pushed up to 10,000 ASA, although at this speed there is a distortion of tonal values and lack of density in the shadows.

Ilford Films

FP4+Microphen. If the light is good enough to operate at around 200 ASA, then this combination will produce high-quality results. It is a very easy combination to use. Develop for 7 minutes in undiluted Microphen for punchy development. Alternatively, dilute 1+1 and process for up to 8 minutes, discarding developer after use.

HP4+Microphen. Dilute 1+3 and process for 12 minutes for speed of 800 ASA. You can experiment with this combination to achieve some amazing increases in speed. An ASA rating of 10,000 (!) has been *claimed* using HP4 and Microphen. Quality obviously suffers but it could prove a life-saver under some circumstances.

When pushing film speeds much above 3200 ASA you are out on your own, and if you ruin the negatives it can't be blamed on the manufacturers. Work very cleanly. Wash all containers carefully to avoid chemical contamination, and be especially careful with tank spirals. These can easily become contaminated with fixer from a previous processing session. Always wash spirals well before putting them out to dry. Before you use them, just touch the tip of your tongue to the inside of the spiral. If it tastes acid or bitter then the spiral is dirty.

COLOUR FOR ACTION

Films such as Kodachrome II which are manufacturer processed (the processing cost is included in the price paid for them) must be rated as specified. You cannot ask the laboratory to increase the speed by forced development. As Kodachrome II is a slow film (25 ASA), it is only suitable for action under the most favourable lighting conditions, although if you can use it, the results will be very rewarding. Many photographers regard this colour transparency film as producing the most subtle and superb results on any stock available.

A more usual film for action work is High Speed Ektachrome. The recommended ASA rating is 160, but this can be increased by forced processing techniques. You can either process at home or send it to a laboratory. If you send it out, then the speed at which it has been rated must be given or the technicians will process at the manufacturer's rating.

Many professionals who are shooting both black and white and colour on the same assignment use High Speed Ektachrome rated to 400 ASA to match the Tri-X stock in their other camera. This makes exposure setting more straightforward and foolproof. High Speed Ektachrome can be rated up to 160 ASA very effectively and I have seen transparencies pushed as high as 4000 ASA. There was an inevitable increase in grain size and a shift in colour balance, but for some action subjects this may be less important than getting an image at all. If in doubt about the film's exposure, 'tag' process – or tell the laboratory to do this for you. A small clip of film is test processed to check the time required. Adjustments are then made when needed.

Developers suitable for action-photography

DEVELOPER	CHARACTERISTICS	MANUFACTURER
Microphen	Fine grain with increase film speed. Clean working, long life. Supplied as a powder. Can be used diluted.	Ilford
Neofin Red	Formulated for use with fast films. Gives good grain structure.	Tetenal
D76	General purpose, fine-grain developer. Produces good image sharpness. Can be replenished. Use 1 − 1 on undiluted.	Kodak
DK50	Fast working developer used to process 2475 Recording Estar. Can be replenished. Used 1 + 1 or diluted.	Kodak
Promicrol	Offers fine grain, increased emulsion speed and replenishment to 50 per cent.	May and Baker
Acu-1	Gives fine grain with high speed. Tri-X can be rated at 1200 ASA, HP4 at 1000 ASA	Phago Photographic

Acufine	Combines fine-grain with high speed. i.e. HP4 can be rated at 1600 ASA. Can be used to push slower emulsions (i.e. FP4) to fast speeds for action work under poor light.	Phago Photographic
Diafine	Two bath developer. Used within temperature range 70°–85°F. Tri-X can be used at 2400 ASA. Claimed to produce highest speeds with lowest grain and best definition.	Phago Photographic
Astronol	High definition developer for fast films. Gives some increase in film speed. Dilute 1+9.	Photax

Black and white films for action photography

TYPE	CHARACTERISTICS	SPEED	SIZE
Agfa Isopan	Fast film, fine grain,	400 ASA	35 mm. 36 exp.
Ultra	high definition.		35 mm. 5 metres 120/620/127
Ilford HP4	Medium contrast, high speed fine grain film.	400 ASA	All sizes
Kodak Tri-X Pan	Wide exposure latitude, very fast, fine grain film.	400 ASA	All sizes
2475 Recording Film	Ultra-fast, but grainy. Only used when nothing else will get the picture.	1600 ASA upwards	35 mm. only

Colour films for action photography

TYPE	CHARACTERISTICS	SPEED	SIZE
Kodak Ektachrome-X	Bright colours. Tends towards the blue on bright days. User process.	64	All sizes

High Speed Ektachrome	Pleasant, soft colours. Can be pushed to high ASA speed. User process.	160 ASA	35 mm. and 120
Kodacolor X	Medium-fast film for colour negatives. User process.	80	Most
GAF Ansco D200	Fast colour film, medium grain.	200	35 mm. 20 and 36 exp.
D500	Ultra-fast colour film tends to be very grainy.	500	35 mm. 20 and 36 exp.

The above charts should be used as a guide only. The best way of discovering the film/processing combination which works best for your type of action photography is by trying a range of material for yourself. But once you have found the combination which gives the kind of results you want, the best advice is to stick with it. Photographers who are constantly changing their film and developers tend to produce uneven results.

Summary
1   When light level is too low to produce required shutter speed/f-stop combination for action work, or you require more contrast, uprate the film. This can be done fairly easily with black and white film. With reversal colour it is harder.
2   Only colour film which can be processed at home or by a trade laboratory can be uprated.
3   Increasing development time also increases grain, contrast and fog level.
4   Keep processing solutions at same temperature to minimise grain size.
5   On days when light level is adequate for shutter speed/f-stop combination required, but contrast is low and dull, under-expose deliberately and increase development time to push up contrast without increasing negative density.

CHAPTER SIX

Lighting for Action Photography

There are three sources of light for general photography:
1 Available light.
2 Flash – electronic or bulb.
3 Tungsten.
So far as action photography is concerned, we are only concerned with the first two sources. The amount of tungsten light which would be needed to light even fairly small subjects satisfactorily for action photography makes it impractical. Even if you had a budget – and a power supply – big enough to produce tens of thousands of watts of tungsten illumination, this would be a wasteful and inefficient way of lighting for action. When the level of available light is too low to achieve the shutter speed/f-stop combination necessary to capture fast action, then the best alternative is electronic flash.

AVAILABLE LIGHT
If the level of available light is high enough to give the shutter speed and f-stop required, then this is the most convenient source.

When the level of available light is low for action shooting, it may still be necessary to use it – and push the film speed – when:
a   it is impractical to light the subject by any other means – for example, when shooting mid-field play in a football match;
b   flash has been prohibited by the organisers of the event—for example, at a gymnastics event where the use of flash might harm the competitor's concentration;
c   the atmosphere produced by the available light is important – for example, when photographing ballet or other stage action.

When shooting under low available light conditions it may be necessary not only to increase the film speed by forced development, but to use some of the techniques described in Chapter Four to obtain action shots at slow shutter speeds; panning the camera for Type One, side-to-side action and catching up-and-down (Type Two) action at the peak of movement.

When shooting on black and white stock, you can help to give the final print more impact by taking care over subject and background contrasts. The use of a slightly long focal length lens (for example, 80 mm. or 135 mm. on 35 mm. format) will help put the background out of focus. Combine this differential focus technique with the juxtaposition of tonal contrasts.

For example, you know that a player's face is going to reproduce light or mid-grey on a black and white print. If you select your angle incorrectly, this grey tone may be caught against a similar grey background tone, making the subject hard to distinguish and thus lowering the impact of the shot. If you select your camera position carefully it should be possible to find a darker grey or black tone in the background so that the subject stands out more boldly. For example, suppose you are photographing a football match. A low angle from one position catches players jumping for a ball against the late afternoon sky. If the sky is overcast, the tone of the players' flesh and the tone of the sky are going to be very close on the final print. By changing position it may be possible to use the dark shape of the stands in the background. At once your picture looks bolder and more dramatic. It will, of course, be necessary to throw the background out of focus by using the suggested long lens with a wide f-stop, but if the light level is

PLATE 49
Problems of contrast caused a delay of 24 hours in shooting this 'one-off' sequence of the car which almost flew. Dark rocks and a black car made it hard to separate foreground and background. Nikon motorised camera 135 mm. lens. 1/1000th second f8. Film rated at 800 ASA to increase contrast. (See also Chapter Five.)

low you will almost certainly be using a wide aperture in any case.

It is sometimes rather hard to judge how the different colours in life will reproduce on a black and white photograph. This ability comes with experience, but at first you may find it easier to judge tone values if you study the scene through half closed eye-lids. This tends to reduce colour values and allow you to see objects in terms of shape and tone.

If the contrast is low and you have control over the subject, it may be better to delay the shooting session until the quality, if not the quantity, of the light improves. I remember some years ago being sent to photograph a stunt in which a car, fitted with wings and a propeller, was being 'flown' off the side of a quarry. It was a complicated affair involving more than 50 people, including a dozen skin-divers who would help free the driver when the car finished up in the bottom of the quarry under 40 ft. of cold, black water.

The car was painted black and the area surrounding the quarry was dark rock. On the day I was supposed to shoot the stunt, the light quantity was just about sufficient for the exposure which I needed – 1/1000th second f5.6 at 800 ASA—but the quality of the light was dismal, dull, flat and grey. Because I was taking the picture for reproduction in newspapers I had to have reasonable contrast on the negative to get a print which could be published on poor quality

PLATE 50
End of the flying car's flight. The driver was trapped for nine minutes before divers could free him. A bottle of air saved his life. Careful exposure/processing techniques saved the assignment.

newsprint. Even from a low angle, which I wanted anyhow in order to emphasise the height of the car at the moment of 'take off', I could not do the obvious and catch the dark shape of the car against the light grey of the sky, because of the high surrounding walls of dark rock.

This was strictly a one-off job with no chance of a retake. So, despite the protests and the problems, I abandoned the shooting session until the following day. The next morning the *quantity* of the light was the same as before, but the *quality* had picked up a little. There was just that tiny increase in contrast which I so badly needed.

The meter exposure reading was 1/1000th second at f5.6, but I shot the pictures on a 135 mm. lens at 1/1000th second f8. By going down that extra stop I was able to increase the film development and so push up the contrast without making the negative over dense. The contrast was still low, but sufficiently good to enable newspaper reproduction. Incidentally, before taking the car pictures I shot off a few frames of another roll of film. This was later cut into small sections in the darkroom. Each section was processed separately, before the crucial roll went through the tank. By inspecting the test strips it was possible to select the processing time which gave the best possible combination of contrast, density and grain. This is a technique which can be usefully adopted whenever a very important action sequence has to be shot (see also tagging of colour film, Chapter Five).

FLASH – GENERAL CONSIDERATIONS

Electronic flash guns are relatively inexpensive and every serious photographer should have one on the equipment schedule. Flash-bulb guns are initially cheaper than even the lowest price electronic gun, but the cost per shot rises sharply if you take a number of flash pictures. For action work, especially sequence photography, a more serious drawback is the time wasted changing bulbs. If you are using flash bulbs and experience wasted shots due to bulb misfire, then try this trick. Place the wire contacts of a capless bulb between your teeth and gently scrape them, then moisten them with your lips before putting the bulb into the gun. Frequently, misfires are due to corrosion on the contacts and this scraping, moistening technique prevents them.

Synchronisation problems

In Chapter One I mentioned that problems can arise when synchronising electronic flash with SLR cameras fitted with focal plane shutters.

This is because, except at fairly slow speeds, the focal plane shutter exposes the negative in a series of strips. A slit in the blind travels across the negative. Thus one end of the frame is exposed a split-second before the other end. A between-the-lens (Compur) shutter works on a different principle. Thin metal leaves open and close under the tension of springs. The tighter the tension the faster they open and close. This places a top limit on the shutter speed possible (1/500th second) but it means that the whole negative is exposed at the same time, even at the fastest possible speed.

The flash from the tube of an electronic gun is virtually instantaneous. If you attempt to synchronise this type of gun with a focal plane shutter above the recommended shutter speed, then only that portion of the negative which was uncovered by the blind during the duration of the flash will be exposed. The rest will be completely black on the print. The only way to successfully synchronise a focal plane shutter to electronic flash is to do so at a speed slow enough for the whole negative area to be exposed at the same time. In practice this means 1/60th second (and on a few cameras, such as the Nikkormat, 1/125th second).

With a Compur shutter, electronic flash can be synchronised at any speed as the leaf shutter uncovers the whole negative at the same time.

In practice the slow synchronisation speed for the focal plane shutter can produce a number of difficulties. In general photography, these are mainly concerned with synchro-sunlight technique, where the subject is back-lit by the sun and detail obtained in the subject by using flash. Under these conditions a shutter speed of 1/60th second is likely to prove too slow and the level of available light will perhaps require an exposure of 1/250th second or more if the negative is not to be over-exposed.

In action photography this situation rarely arises. But slow synchronisation speeds can lead to different difficulties, which will be discussed in Part Two of this book. These mainly occur when you try to use flash in available light levels which are too low to provide an adequate exposure, yet sufficient to produce an image on the negative. This can lead to a ghosting effect, with the main part of the picture, taken by flash, being duplicated by a blurred available-light picture.

One way around the problem is to use focal plane flash bulbs when photographing this type of subject. Focal plane bulbs are very long burning compared with ordinary bulbs. They can be synchronised with focal plane shutters at the highest speeds because they give out their light over a long enough period for the slit in the shutter to travel across the whole negative area.

Electronic flash

In some action situations the flash head must be used close to the camera position, but this produces flat, uninteresting lighting and should be avoided whenever possible. If you cannot bounce the flash from some suitable reflector to produce a softer, more natural effect (see below), try and put the light in at an angle by using a long synch. lead and holding the flash in the hand rather than having it bolted on to the side of the camera.

An unpleasant characteristic of single flash illumination is the dense, dark backgrounds which are produced. Subjects often seem to be emerging from a pitch black night. You can overcome this problem, and produce more pleasing pictures, by using a second flash head to one side of, or behind, the subject. This flash head is best held by an assistant who can move it around as the action changes. As it is usually difficult or impractical to synchronise this second flash gun with a connecting lead, use a slave trigger to fire it.

The technique is as follows. Fix one gun to the camera – when two sources are being used, one can be fitted on to a camera shoe or bar to provide fill-in illuminations. The other light is held by an assistant at 45° to the camera to provide modelling, or from behind the subject (taking care that it does not intrude into the picture area) to provide rim lighting. Both effects will produce far more dramatic and eye-catching pictures than the single flash technique.

Bounce flash

Where fast-moving subjects or large areas are involved, bounce flash,

PLATE 51
Bounce electronic flash provides a high speed light source which will 'freeze' action whilst remaining natural-looking. This stage school's lesson in the art of custard pie throwing was shot on a Hasselblad 500EL with two Solar 4 flash guns

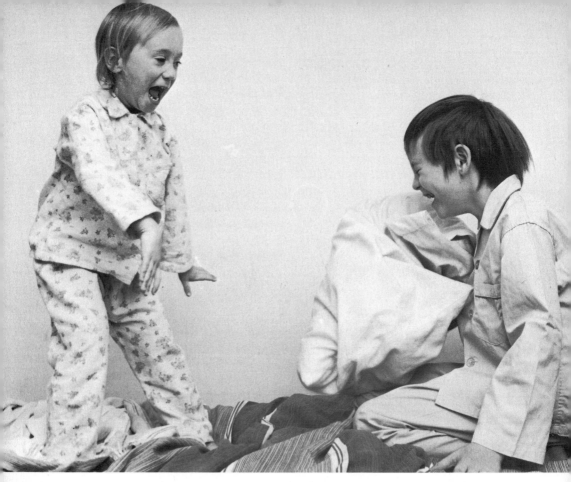

PLATE 52
Bounce flash exposure calculations are easy in small, lightly decorated rooms. Here a direct flash exposure (calculated from the guide number) was f16. The flash was bounced off the opposite wall to the subjects and the f-stop opened to f11

PLATE 53 (opposite)
Twin electronic flash heads were used for this shot. The camera was a Rolleiflex.

whether you reflect the light from a wall or an umbrella, may prove impractical. But use this technique when possible to get more natural, rounded and softer illumination.

Many photographers avoid bounce flash because they believe it is difficult. This is not so. All it involves is turning the flash head so that the light 'bounces' off some suitable reflector, instead of directing the flash at the subject. This may be a wall, the ceiling or a white umbrella. Some light will be lost, especially if the reflecting surface is dark or some distance from the gun, and you must compensate for this by opening up the f-stop. The increase in aperture required for bounce flash work depends on so many variables that it is impossible to lay down anything other than guide lines.

For example, if a flash factor calculation gives an exposure of f16 for direct flash, then when bouncing from a light blue or white wall within 6 ft. of the flash gun, open up by one stop to f11. If the room is very large, a gymnasium perhaps, it will be advisable to open up to f8.

Calculating the f-stop for bounce flash pictures is a matter of experience. Start with black and white film because the exposure latitude is so much better than with colour. Make a note of the direct flash exposure (calculated from the flash factor) and the bounce flash exposure which you gave, plus a brief record of the subject and conditions. When you have processed the negative, note whether it was correctly exposed or not. Keep this notebook with you and it will provide a valuable practical reference to using bounce flash under different conditions. When you can get black and white bounce pictures right, try your hand at colour. When shooting reversal colour, beware of bouncing off coloured walls or ceilings as these will produce a colour cast on the transparency. The best bounce reflector for colour transparencies is a silver or gold umbrella specially designed for this type of photography. Gold adds a warmth to the flesh tones and is mainly used by glamour photographers, but it can make action shots more attractive as well.

If you find difficulty getting bounce colour exposures right, then you will save a great deal of money and wasted film by investing in either a flash meter – which will measure the bounce flash and tell you the correct f-stop to use – or a computerised flash gun (see below).

Typical record book for bounce flash

F-STOP*	PICTURE	BOUNCE F-STOP	RESULT
f16	Basket ball in large hall. Bounced off yellow wall 4 ft. from flash. Total subject-flash distance (4 ft. + 10 ft. = 14 ft.)	f11	Thin, f8 would have been better
f18	Gymnastics. Small gym. Bounce flash off small white umbrella 6 ft. from subject. Total subject – flash distance approx. 16 ft.	f4	Dense f5.6 would have been better

* Calculated from flash factor for direct flash.

Recycling times

After an electronic flash shot has been taken, the gun will need a few seconds to recharge the capacitators. This is termed the recycling period. It varies from less than a second to 20 or more seconds, depending on the design of gun, the state of the batteries and how

PLATE 54 (opposite) This shot could have been taken by tungsten light. But the problems of heat from photoflood bulbs would have made the model's task far less comfortable. Bounce electronic flash was a more satisfactory answer. Picture on a Hasselblad 500EL. Balcar electronic flash with white bounce umbrella much output is being demanded. During this recycling period the photographer is, of course, unable to take any pictures. If shots are attempted, the negative is likely to be seriously under-exposed. Some guns recycle very rapidly, especially at power. If you intend to use a gun for sequence work, then check the recycling time before buying it.

Computerised electronic guns
These guns take the technical headaches of exposure calculation out of the photographer's hands. A photo cell measures light bouncing back from the subject and adjusts the speed of the flash (from between 1/1000th second and 1/50,000th second) to give a correct exposure. These are a boon to the less technically minded, or to any photographer who wants to get good results without working out distances and f-stops. Some designs can be used with bounce flash technique. Because they offer such a high speed flash when used with subjects which are very close, they can be used to produce some interesting ultra-fast flash shots. Water droplets bursting, aerosol sprays firing, the moment when a light bulb shatters, can all be frozen to produce pictures which, a few years ago, would have required thousands of pounds-worth of sophisticated electronics and been well outside the scope of most photographers.

PLATES 55–57 (below and opposite) This sequence of pictures showing a chameleon about to snatch his greenfly breakfast was taken with a computerised electronic gun. Fast recycling time and very high speed enabled the whole drama to be captured.

Summary

Electronic flash is the best light source for action. The high speed of the flash tube (1/1000th second upwards) helps to freeze action. It is compact and easily transported.

Electronic flash synchronisation with focal plane shutters can present some problems. Focal plane flash bulbs are sometimes the answer. Use two flash heads whenever possible. Synchronise the second head with a slave trigger device.

Use bounce flash to provide a soft, even illumination.

Computerised flash guns automatically calculate the correct exposure and vary the flash speed to adjust for different subject-flash distances. They are especially useful for colour transparency shooting where exposures are critical. Some designs may also be used for bounce flash technique.

The high-speed flash produced by these guns when photographing objects close at hand will enable you to take some unusual, ultra-fast shots.

CHAPTER SEVEN

Motorised Cameras

Motorised cameras enable the photographer to do two things which would be impossible with any other type of camera:

1   Take a rapid sequence of pictures – up to 9 frames per second on standard cameras, 50 frames per second on the very specialised Hulcher High Speed Camera (see below).

2   Take several pictures from a distance, using either an electrical release or radio control.

The scope for action shooting, given these two facilities, is enormously increased. Let me give you some examples.

Recently I was asked to take pictures at a bomb disposal training school. Amongst the gadgets being demonstrated was a self-igniting Molotov cocktail, the sort of thing which gets used with such devastating effect by urban guerrillas. I wanted a close-up shot of one of these devices exploding into flames the moment it struck a wall. I would never have been given permission to stand right in the path of the spurting flames – even if I had been crazy enough to try, and my dedication to the 'different' picture does have its limitations! But nobody had the slightest objections to my placing a motorised Nikon in the firing line. An NCO checked the bottle which struck the wall and burst into flames. I fired the camera from a safe distance using radio control equipment. The result – a picture with a difference which helped to sell the story. This ability to 'get a new angle on things' is a valuable one when it comes to marketing actions pictures, as I shall explain in Chapter Nine.

A very different assignment was to photograph an expert diver in such a way that each stage of a complicated spring-board dive could be analysed. Only a motorised camera could have captured the type of high-speed sequence, (see pages 107–109).

On another occasion I had to photograph a driver trying to leap his car across a river. When the intended stunt had been described to me, I thought it would look more dramatic if we had a fisherman in a boat underneath the flying car. A local angler was sitting in a small craft not far away and he was persuaded to move his boat up-river. The driver assured him that his car would easily clear the water and land on the opposite bank. Unfortunately, the car hit the jumping ramps too slowly and landed in the water, narrowly missing the fishing boat. The angler,

PLATE 58
A radio control
motorised Nikon camera
was used to capture
this shot of a Molotov
cocktail exploding on
impact.

PLATE 59 (opposite,
overleaf and top of
page 109)
Analysis of diving
action made possible
by a motorised Nikon
camera sequence.
Exposure was 1/1000th
second at f4 on a
standard lens

taking no chances as he saw several hundredweight of steel descending on his head, abandoned ship and dived over the side. The driver was unhurt. He pulled himself through the open driver's window without even getting his feet wet and stood on the roof, waving delightedly. But the soaked and infuriated fisherman wasn't going to let him get away so lightly. He hauled himself out of the river, clambered on to the car and socked the driver in the face, sending him flying backwards into the river. My first shots had been made with a 28 mm. wide angle lens on the motorised Nikon. I had just changed to a 135 mm. lens, to catch the car as it floated away down the river, when I saw the driver pulling himself on to the car. There was just time to raise, focus, fire and capture the perfect end picture for my story. Thanks to the motor, I had got a picture feature which sold around the world (see pages 109–112).

PLATES 60–65 (left and pages 110–112)
A car tries to fly across a river and an angler takes an impromptu bath. A sequence which could only have been taken with a motorised camera.

One final assignment will demonstrate something of the versatility of the motor-drive camera. My instructions were to photograph a group of stunt men who spend their spare moments keeping in stunting trim by dropping bombs on each other. What happened was this. One stunt man would pilot a Tiger Moth, while his companion climbed out on to a wing. The volunteer 'target' sprinted across a field, chased by the plane. When they were overhead the man on the wing dropped a 'bomb' made mostly from cardboard and filled with a small explosive charge. If it hit the 'target' it splashed his padded coat with a dye and he was considered 'dead'.

A good story but a tough one to photograph. How could I show the connection between the aircraft, the man on the wing and the man on the ground in a single, dramatic picture? My solution was to mount the motorised camera on the tail of the Tiger Moth, using a specially made-up bracket. The actual picture was taken by the pilot who used a micro-switch release taped to his control column. In the photograph you can see the cable which connected the camera to the switch trailing along the edge of the aircraft. The camera was fitted with a 28 mm. wide angle lens (and a prayer shawl!).

In Part Two of this book you will see further suggestions for the ways in which motorised cameras can be used to obtain pictures with a difference.

Some photographers don't understand the difference between shooting with a motor-drive camera and using a cine-camera. I have been asked before now why a movie camera couldn't be used for this type of work. The answer is that a cine camera shutter takes a picture at about 1/40th second. If you were to examine individual frames of some fast-action sequence, you would find that each picture was blurred. It is only when they are projected at the correct speed that they *appear* sharp. Motorised cameras can take their sequence pictures at up to 1/2000th second on conventional cameras and up to 1/10,000 second on the Hulcher High Speed Camera.

When covering a sports subject the motor enables a photographer to record a sequence of actions and then select the best frames from his negatives to print up. This ability to edit and enlarge from a selection of pictures taken within split-seconds of each other is extremely useful when covering fast-moving events. It is, ironically enough, the main argument against the use of motor-drives put forward by some

PLATE 66

Picture taken by motorised Nikon mounted on tail-plane of Tiger Moth aircraft. The pilot fired the shutter via a cable release and a micro-switch fitted to the joystick. The firing cable can be seen leading from the bottom left of the picture. Aircraft was fifteen feet above the ground. Exposure (preset!) 1/1000th second f8

photographers. They claim that, by relying on his motor-drive to capture the sequence of events, the photographer is no longer in command of the situation. That vital 'moment of truth', which French photo-journalist Henri Cartier Bresson identified as the key to a great picture, becomes a matter of chance. If the camera happens to be winding on the film when this 'moment of truth' occurs, then the picture will be lost for ever. I agree that this may happen. But for every missed picture the photographer with a motor-drive system will catch a hundred he might otherwise have missed.

Hulcher high speed camera
This is probably the ultimate high-speed sequence camera for general photography. Made by Charles A. Hulcher and Co. Inc. of Hampton, Virginia, the camera uses a semi-silvered mirror to provide continuous viewing and taking through the same lens. This system, which has been used occasionally in more conventional 35 mm. cameras, avoids the need for a moving mirror, but there is considerable light loss. In practice you need to open up by around 2 stops. The Hulcher is powered by a battery pack similar to that used by news film photographers. It will take 50 frames per second at a wide range of shutter speeds up to 1/10,000 second. This is a very specialist piece of equipment, a fact reflected by the price and the problems of using it. When handled by an expert it can produce remarkable action pictures.

AT A GLANCE GUIDE TO POPULAR MOTORISED CAMERAS

TYPE	FRAMES PER SECOND RANGE	INTEGRAL OR PURCHASED SEPARATELY	POWER SUPPLY
Canon	4–9 fps	Integral.	Rechargeable and penlight.
Contax	2 fps (5 fps with heavy duty batteries)	Separate. No adjustment needed to camera.	Penlight on heavy duty cells for 5 fps.
Nikon F	2–4 fps	Separate. Cameras have to be adjusted to take motor.	Penlight.
Nikon F2	1–5 fps	Separate. No adjustment needed. Can be quickly removed for manual operation of camera.	Rechargeable and penlight.
Olympus	1–5 fps	Separate. No adjustment needed.	Rechargeable and penlight.
Pentax	3 fps	Separate.	Rechargeable and penlight.

TRIGGERING SYSTEMS

One of the most interesting things about owning a motor-drive camera is dreaming up ways of triggering it so as to produce new picture-taking possibilities. Here are 4 of the methods which I and other magazine photo-journalists have used.

Radio control

The camera is fitted with a radio receiver similar to that used by model aircraft enthusiasts. With a suitable transmitter the photographer can stand up to a mile away and trigger his camera. The camera may be set either for sequence or single picture work. In the latter mode, the transmitter triggers the shutter and then winds on the film ready for the next shot. I used radio control, for example, to photograph a fighter aircraft testing out a gravel pit arrester. This was a long trench filled with shingle which was developed to bring to a safe halt aircraft which overshot the runway for any reason. A camera with a wide angle lens was mounted right on the arrested bed and recorded a dramatic sequence of pictures as the fighter thundered towards it.

PLATE 69
A young artist painted on blown up motor cars. The photographer's job was to record this explosive feat. This picture was easy; a wide angle lens on a Nikon camera. But photographing the explosion itself required more complicated equipment (see Plate 70)

Cable

This is an ordinary flex fitted with a micro-switch to close the circuit. I have used these successfully up to 100 yds distance.

Pressure pads and trip wires

I have used these abroad to photograph wild animals. A simple pressure pad, made from two sheets of plywood with brass contacts held apart by a small foam rubber pad, is buried in the path to a water hole. The animal then takes its own picture. Trip wires, fine lines of cotton, are useful for small, light animals.

Sound triggers

During the American moon programme, cameras fitted with sound switches were used to record various stages of lift-off. The switches were built so that they triggered the camera when a certain level of sound was reached. This allowed the photographers to take sequence pictures automatically at any stage of the lift-off by consulting with NASA engineers on noise levels.

CHAPTER EIGHT

Getting to Where the Action is . . .

Very often, getting your camera within lens range of a subject is much harder than taking the actual pictures! I have spent days, weeks on one occasion, trying to persuade the various officials who had to give their blessing to allow me to take the photographs I wanted, and this with the supposed 'advantages' of a press card and a big magazine name as proof of my professionalism!

The beginner, or the more experienced amateur starting up in action photography for the first time, may find many subjects ruled out, not by lack of ability or the right equipment, but merely because red-tape and rules prevent him from getting close enough to the action.

Many photographers in this position may be forgiven for thinking that a press card is the open sesame solution to their problems. Only now and then is this true. To get into a really big sporting event, for example, you will need more than a piece of pasteboard proclaiming membership of the National Union of Journalists; you will need special passes, authorisations, clearances and enough paper work on some occasions to gladden the heart of petty bureaucrats the world over.

There are no hard and fast rules for getting into places. Some events are easier to cover than others, some are impossible unless you work for a major magazine, newspaper or agency. By impossible I only mean *impossible* to get special positions from which to shoot your pictures. This doesn't mean that coverage is out of the question. In his early days, Ed Lacey, now regarded as one of the finest sports photographers in Europe, faced constant problems when he wanted to get his cameras close to the action. He never let this deter him. He never let official rudeness or stupidity put him off, and eventually his persistence won through. An enthusiastic amateur for years, Ed turned professional when he realised that he was making more money from his weekend sports photography than from his regular job. But even as a professional he faced difficulties. In 1964, just after he had gone into full-time sports photography, he decided to fly out to Tokyo to cover the Olympic Games. He could only work from the public stands because he had no arena pass. As an amateur he had often let officials bully him off the course. But in Tokyo, with his airfare and expenses to pay for and new-found boldness which came from his professional status, Ed was not so easily moved on. 'I would find my seat, dump my camera cases and move

PLATE 71 (opposite) You don't need a special pass to get good pictures. Ed Lacey covered the 1964 Olympic Games in Tokyo from the public stands and caught shots like this by using long lenses. 800 mm. lens on Nikon camera.

PLATE 72
A long lens can often replace the hard-to-get special pass. A spectator stand shot at Hickstead made with an 800 mm. lens on a Nikon camera.

around where I wanted,' he recalls. 'I was still on the spectators' side of the barrier but going around the area to get the right viewpoints. Japanese officials kept on coming to pester me, but fortunately the only English they knew was: 'You got pass?' I just said 'Yes, thanks' and kept on taking pictures and writing down caption notes. In the end they got fed up and walked away.'

Starting out
Organisers of hill climbs, stock-car races, local football matches, minor air shows and so on will usually be sympathetic to your request for passes to special positions, the arena or touch-line, if you are able to offer them something in return. What you can offer are free photographs and the chance of publicity.

Do not try and start at the big events. For one thing your action shooting technique may not be up to it. If you manage to talk your way into a prime position at some important event and then produce a disappointing set of pictures the officials are probably not going to give

PLATE 73
A scoop picture (see Chapter Ten) taken by an amateur photographer in the crowd at an air show. His quick shutter finger beat every other cameraman there, professional and amateur, when a Vulcan exploded in a mid-air disaster.

you the same chance again. So cut your teeth on minor events; amateur football matches, local car club meetings and that kind of thing. Produce a good portfolio and make sure that the photographs are professionally presented and printed.

When you feel confident about your photographic ability and want to tackle something more important, contact the organisers of the events concerned. The best person to speak to is usually the club secretary, or the organising secretary if it is a fairly small, local event. If it is a much bigger event, then they may have a man dealing specifically with press and publicity. He can be a valuable ally if approached in the right way. Remember that his job will be to get the event maximum publicity. If you persuade him that you can do this (see Chapter Nine) then he will be much more likely to co-operate. Unless you go to the trouble of having printed notepaper and typing your letters, it will be best to make the first approach by phone. Always plan your coverage well in advance. Do not turn up with the crowds and expect special treatment or any concessions just because you are carrying a camera. You will find the first 12 months the hardest, because after that you will be approaching organisers of annual events for the second time around. If you have done a good job for them the year before, and sent off the set of complimentary prints which you promised, then they will be much more likely to help you. As your name gets known, more and more doors will open to you.

The essential thing is not to abuse special privileges by taking advantage of them or by acting in a dangerous manner. For example, if you get special permission to cover a stock-car meeting from the centre of the arena, don't take this as an invitation to bring your wife and children along too. If a race marshall asks you not to stand in a particular place because it may endanger the drivers, then don't go back there as soon as he has moved away.

If you decide to take up action photography professionally, even on a part-time basis, then have notepaper and business cards printed. Keep the printing simple and sophisticated. It will be sufficient, for example, to say: 'J. Bloggs – Sports Photographer' or something along these lines. There is no need for anything else except your address and phone number.

Example of the type of letter which might be written to the organiser of a sports event to obtain a pass or special concessions for photography.

Dear Sir,

I see from an advertisement in the local press that you are organising an autocross event in this area.

I am a local freelance sports photographer contributing pictures to the

PLATE 74 (opposite) Shots of this sort of quality taken at amateur events will please both contestants and organisers and could win you special permissions for the next event local and national press and specialist magazines.

I would like to cover this event and wonder if you would be good enough to supply me with a track pass so that I can get the best possible pictures. I will, of course, be happy to provide your club with a set of complimentary photographs of the event for your records.

Yours faithfully,

If you recover some of your operating costs by selling pictures to magazines and newspapers, then collect cuttings of the published material. They will help to convince organisers and publicity men that you can be valuable to them.

Prints are a useful passport into the good books of players, participants and organisers alike. Don't be mean. At first give away as many well-printed photographs as you can afford. If the clubs or individuals want to place orders for further prints, then of course you can charge them. But organisers will often expect at least one set of free prints.

Working from the public stands
Some events are so exclusive that no amount of writing or persuasion will get you a prime camera position, unless you get a job for a major newspaper or agency. Don't let this worry you. With long lenses and a well-chosen vantage point in the public stands it is still possible to get excellent pictures. If possible, make a visit to the arena, stadium or area of operations prior to the event. Use visual anticipation to plan a coverage and select the best position. Bear in mind the position of the sun during the time you will be shooting pictures (I carry a small compass around with me on these reconnaissance trips just for this purpose). If numbered seats can be reserved, then make sure you get the one you want by booking well in advance. If it is a case of first come first served, turn up early enough to get the position which you have chosen. If you go with a friend he may be able to keep one vantage point for you while you go to another good position. Be very careful about leaving camera equipment lying around though, even under the 'eye' of a friendly spectator. Carry all your equipment with you at all times.

Summary
1   Organisers of events will help you if you can help them with good pictures of the event and/or publicity.
2   Plan any coverage well in advance. Contact the secretary or person specially responsible for press and publicity.

3   Start with unimportant events and work up. Do not spoil your chances later by tackling a coverage for which you are technically unprepared.

4   Always provide the prints you have promised. Failure to do so will breed ill-will and the door may not open to you a second time around.

CHAPTER NINE

Selling Action Pictures

Selling action pictures to magazines and newspapers can have a number of advantages for the serious photographer – not the least being an extra income to offset the high cost of photography. Apart from the useful extra cash, and the pleasure of seeing one's work published, a scrap book of cuttings can prove, as I mentioned in the last chapter, a useful passport to the more important sporting events. The chance of good publicity is bait which few organisers can resist. But many would-be contributors to the press are soon discouraged by the inevitable rejection slips which greet many of their early offerings. This can very often arise from a lack of knowledge about marketing pictures. Before going on to discuss the various publications which will buy action photographs, therefore, it will be useful to look briefly at the reasons why editors reject material.

1   *They have no budget for buying freelance contributions.*

This applies only to very small, limited circulation magazines and some provincial newspapers where the editor has no spare cash to buy from outside sources.

2   *The story has already been covered by a staff photographer or a retained freelance contributor; or they have received it from another outside source, i.e. an agency or established freelance who regularly supplies them with material.*

There is very little that you can do about this, except watch out for other cameramen when you are taking your own pictures and try to discover who they are shooting for.

3   *The story has already been covered by the magazine in a previous issue.*

This can be avoided by market research. You must study several copies of a magazine to which you intend to supply material. Far too many freelances blithely send their work to magazines knowing nothing more about the market than the title and address gleaned from some reference book. It can be very irritating for a busy editor to receive a potentially useful contribution on a subject which has already be exhaustively dealt with in his pages. You can, of course, blunder without realising it. Because most magazines work several issues ahead you may send in material on a subject which they have already covered but not yet published.

4 *The story is unsuitable for the magazine concerned.*

Market research again. Could your pictures ever appear in that particular magazine? By doing research at the local library over a period of weeks, taking a subscription for the magazine or merely buying occasional copies, you will soon find out.

5 *The story is technically poor.*

Frequently, when I was a feature agency picture editor, I received stories which I would very much liked to have bought, but the standard of photography was too poor. Very few photographers are sufficiently objective about the quality of their work. Learn to stand back and view your pictures with the dispassionate eye of a man who is going to have to pay good money for them. Ask yourself these questions:

a Are the negatives as sharp as they could reasonably be expected to be?

b Is the definition good enough for reproduction in a magazine or newspaper?

c Are the prints of a professional standard?

d Are the angles interesting enough? (Check with pictures published in the magazine concerned.)

e Are there sufficient pictures to tell the story?

6 *The subject matter is too local or too dull for a nationally distributed magazine or newspaper.*

Because an event has been a big attraction in one's home town, one can get an exaggerated sense of its interest to those who do not know the people involved. With experience you will soon be able to judge the likely interest. Market research will help greatly in acquiring a national perspective on local events.

As you can see there may be a number of reasons why material gets rejected. The main thing for a freelance contributor is not to get discouraged. Learn from your rejection slips. When material is returned, try and discover which of the six reasons stated above is likely to have been the cause. Only very rarely will the editor of the magazine bother to write and tell you. Editors tend to be overworked men and women, especially on local papers or specialist magazines. If they do bother to write, then read what they have to say carefully. It may be a sign that they would like to receive more, but in some way different, material from you.

Sending out material

The first stage, when you return from an action assignment, is to process your negatives and contact print them. A contact print enables you to see each picture in relation to the next, and to study the whole negative area. 35 mm. film can be contacted on a single sheet of 10 in. × 8 in. paper after being cut into strips of 6; roll film should be cut into appropriate strips for printing on a single sheet. For example, 120 film with 12 exposures can be cut into strips of either 3 or 4. Either use a sheet of heavy plate glass to hold the negatives flat on the paper, or a commercially made strip printer.

When the contact sheet is dry, study it carefully. Earlier, I mentioned that it was often impossible to know exactly what you have shot when covering high-speed action. There may be a first-class picture on the roll which you have no recollection of ever taking. Use a magnifying glass to examine each frame. See how the pictures can be masked down to remove unwanted foregrounds or to eliminate obtrusive backgrounds. Two L-shaped sheets of black card may be used for this purpose. The contact sheet can be marked with a chinagraph pencil to indicate how you should print it. Remember the power of the diagonal line in composition to suggest movement. Sometimes it is possible to add drama to a shot by printing it at a slight angle. I advise you to use a black chinagraph, as red or yellow marks are hard to see under darkroom safelight illumination.

The next stage is to make the prints from your marked-up negatives. The standard size for submission to the press is 10 in. × 8 in. on glossy, but not necessarily glazed, paper. If you have only a small glazer and don't get a very even glaze, then it is better to dry the prints with a matt finish.

When the prints are dry you may like to remove any small white specks, caused by dust on the enlarger carrier or the negative itself, with a fine brush and some watercolour lightly applied. Get a book on print finishing and practise this skill on dud prints before trying your hand at an important job. There is no need to do any other type of retouching, nor should you worry too much about a few small specks. If the print is very spotted, however, it will probably be easier to make a fresh print, after carefully dusting down the glass carrier and the film.

If you are taking up freelance action press photography seriously, then a rubber stamp may be a useful investment. This must carry your name, address and telephone number. There is no need for it to say 'Copyright Photograph'. The fact that you took the picture gives you legal protection without the need to state the fact. When you have stamped a batch of prints, keep them separate until the ink has dried or you may stain some of the pictures and have the chore of re-printing.

If you are sending the pictures to a newspaper or magazine it is *essential* to include a caption note. The captions may be handwritten, in block capitals preferably, provided they are short. But if you want to send lengthy captions or a short article, it must be typed. Use double-spacing on one side of the paper only and keep a carbon for your own reference. Individual captions can be fixed to the back of the prints with Sellotape or a non-staining paste.

Captions
These should answer the following questions:

What is happening?	The event.
Where did it happen?	Location of event.
To whom did it happen?	Those involved, names, ages if possible, addresses.
How did it happen?	The reason for the event.
Why did it happen?	The reason for the incident depicted.

I have written an imaginary caption for the photograph shown here (picture 75).

Picture: Joe Bloggs, 2 Market Street, Leicester. Telephone Leicester 1234. 'A mud wrestling bout which took place on Monday, 3rd July at Syston, near Leicester, was interrupted by an angry spectator. The bout was being staged at the annual fair between the Masked Invader and the

PLATE 75
A moment of unexpected excitement at a mud wrestling match could mean sales for the alert freelance. Caption for this picture shown in text

Boston Strangler when housewife Mrs. Julie White (23) of Barnard Street, Leicester, jumped up into the ring to attack the Boston Strangler (real name Fred Bloggs, 22, from London). A crowd of several hundred watched as Julie White attacked the wrestler. She was later escorted from the ring: "I do not know what came over me," said Mrs. White, a mother of two children, later. "He was fighting dirty and I just lost my temper." The Boston Strangler refused to comment after the bout, which he lost by two falls.' (Ends)

This would give a caption writer sufficient material to prepare a brief note to go beneath the picture. Note that in addition to the bare bones of what; where; when; why; etc., I have added a quote from the person mainly involved. I have her address so that I will be able to contact her again if I need more details at a later date.

Sending material off
Everything is now ready for despatch. The prints have been made, the caption notes written or typed, and a possible market for the material found. The pictures and text are put inside a card-backed envelope together with return postage. There is no need to enclose a covering letter as the material should be self-explanatory. Before posting it a record must be made of where it is being sent and the date. If the material comes back it can then be sent out again, and again if necessary, without the risk of posting it twice to the same magazine. By keeping a note of the date of despatch it will be possible to chase up editors if they keep the material for an undue length of time. About a fortnight is reasonable with a monthly magazine; after that you could send a polite letter asking for a decision or the return of your material.

Records can conveniently be kept on oblong index cards. A typical card might look like this:

Subject	Date Taken	Market	Sent/Returned	
Spill at motor cycle hill climb	12/6	Local press	13/6	16/6
		Motor Cycle Magazine	13/6	Used
		Weekend	15/6	20/6
		House Journal	18/6	Used

Make it clear that your are only offering them *Reproduction Rights* in the pictures. Most small papers, house journals and specialist magazines will not expect to buy anything more than this anyhow.

The other rights which you can sell in a picture are as follows:
1 *First Rights.* You will not offer the same material to any other magazine or newspaper until the editor who has bought First Rights has

used the material. First Rights are usually limited to specific countries. For example, you could sell First British Rights to a magazine and still be free to offer that material in Australia, America or Germany. For the circumstances under which you might offer First Rights, see Chapter Ten.

2 *Exclusive Rights.* You will be unwise to sell exclusive rights on material. If a picture set is so good that a newspaper or magazine offers to buy exclusive world rights, then you will probably make more money selling through an agent. See Chapter Ten.

Return of material

Generally, if you include return postage, a magazine or newspaper should return unused material. However, if they lose it you have no real hope of recompense as they will almost certainly publish a disclaimer in every copy of their magazine pointing out that they accept no responsibility for loss of, or damage to, unsolicited articles. Normally, if they buy and use an article, black and white prints will not be returned. They are either thrown away by the publisher or, more usually, kept in the picture library for possible future use. If they are used again you should, of course, receive another fee.

Colour transparencies should be returned after use. Major picture agencies will only send original colour slides to publications on the understanding that a substantial fee be paid if the material is lost or damaged. Freelances, until they are well established, are not really in a position to make this sort of demand. It's 'a buyer's market'. If you have a really valuable set of colour slides it may be best to get duplicate transparencies made. Send these to the magazine. If they insist on being sent the originals after deciding to buy the material, then agree on condition they accept liability for the loss or damage of the material.

You must be prepared to lose a substantial number of black and white prints each year, through postal errors and mishandling in the editorial offices. It is a part of the price to pay for freelancing.

Now let us look at an actual assignment to see how the material was handled once the pictures had been taken. A showman friend of mine told me that he intended to fire a young girl from a giant fairground cannon. Would I be interested in covering the 'test shot'? If a man had been involved I might have been less enthusiastic, but a girl always helps to sell a set of pictures. The lady had made it clear that she was only prepared to be fired once, so I had to be careful to get *my* shots right the first time. I used a motorised Nikon fitted with a 135 mm. lens and pressed the shutter release as the count down to fire the cannon reached 'two'. Out came the girl in a puff of smoke – and out came something else

as well. Too much explosive had been used and the unlucky lady lost her pants. At the time I wasn't really aware of what was happening, but all became clear when she landed in the net!

When the films had been processed and contact printed I knew that a routine story had turned into one which was likely to make spreads in magazines all over the world. At the time I was working with an agency, so they made up 20 or so sets of 10 in. × 8 in. and 1 set of 15 in. × 12 in. prints. The large prints I would have taken round the Fleet Street picture desks with considerable confidence that I could sell them for a good fee. In the event, they were published over a whole page in the *Sun* newspaper. I would then have offered my 10 in. × 8 in. prints to overseas magazine editors; in fact, I would expect them to come on to me after the *Sun* spread appeared. I would have hoped to sell the pictures in Germany, Italy, and perhaps France, or Scandinavia, Australia and South Africa. I would then have tried American markets, but not been very surprised if they turned them down – after all, America is the land

of stunts. If I had only sold a single picture to the *Sun* I would have tried the full sequence on a general interest magazine, but as they used three pictures this pretty well killed interest in the UK. The fees which you could expect for a well syndicated set of action pictures like these would be in the region of £500.

References for markets
There are two main reference works for freelance photo-journalists which you will find in most public libraries. The first is the very well known: *The Writers' and Artists' Year Book*, published annually by A. and C. Black. It lists major magazines in Britain and overseas, agents who handle picture material, and picture libraries. It has articles dealing with such problems as copyright and the technique for submitting work.

The second book is *Willing's Press Guide*, also published annually by Hutchinson Willing Ltd. of London. This lists every provincial paper in the country and can be a valuable reference work for the freelance. There is also a European guide which gives the titles and addresses of daily papers, periodicals, magazines, trade and specialist publications of all the major countries.

PLATE 79 (opposite)
How a German magazine
featured the incident. A
set of pictures like this
could be expected to
net between £100–£500
for the freelance

The first 2 books are essential reading for every freelance photo-journalist. Remember to study the subjects covered by the magazine before sending them material, or you may commit a similar blunder to the photo-journalist who sent some gory battle pictures to a magazine called *War Cry*. The title may have sounded right to him, but in fact it is the magazine of the Salvation Army!

③

London:
Weltpremiere
mit einer
weiblichen
Kanonenkugel

Voll-treffer mit Dame

CHAPTER TEN

The Markets for Action Photographs

In the last chapter I discussed the techniques for preparing and sending out action photographs. But there is one type of picture which must be dealt with in a completely different way – the scoop picture. You may only get a scoop once or twice in your photographic career, but when it comes you need to know exactly what to do. Before dealing with routine markets for run-of-the-mill action pictures, I want to explain exactly how you should act in order to cash in on your scoop.

Scoop pictures

Where there is action and danger there is always the chance of something going wrong. The scope for getting a world-beating set of pictures in this branch of photography is greater than any other. In a split-second an event of no great interest to anybody except those directly concerned with it may become front page material. Not long ago I was photographing a touring stunt driving show performing at a small, seaside town. I was preparing a magazine spread on the team, but otherwise it would only have attracted local press photographers and, perhaps, an alert local freelance. But the tragic happened. A stunt man was killed. My pictures were in great demand, and one was sold exclusively to a national paper and appeared on the front page.

To take another example, (picture 73): an alert photographer was attending an air show, training his camera on the jets thundering overhead. Suddenly one exploded. There were professionals and amateurs at the show, hundreds of cameras, but his was the only shutter to click at the crucial moment.

These two examples demonstrate that *exclusivity* is the essential ingredient of a scoop picture. A newspaper pays a high price for such a photograph because it is unique, a picture that none of its rivals can get. The split-second of drama captured only in the camera of one quick and fortunate photographer. How much the newspapers are prepared to pay for such a picture will depend on how dramatic it is likely to be, and how important the story.

When the stunt man died, there were two local newspaper photographers apart from myself. But only my camera was focused on the unfortunate man a split-second before his death. So my shots were more dramatic than anybody else's there. Even if they had wanted or been allowed to offer their pictures to a national paper, mine would still

PLATE 80 (top right) A split-second before his fatal accident this stuntman was delighting crowds at a seaside show . . .

PLATE 81 (bottom right) . . . tragedy has struck and the stuntman has been critically injured. These pictures were in great demand by the newspapers as a result of this accident. Death is often the yardstick by which picture editors measure the value of a scoop picture. Nikon camera.

PLATES 82–85 (below, opposite and pages 142–143)
A remarkable action sequence captured by a German cameraman as a racing car spun off the track and was totally wrecked. This was a major scoop sequence which made newspaper and magazine publications around the world. Astonishingly the driver stepped out unhurt as the final picture (Plate 85) shows

have beaten them. In the second example, the photographer had a more important scoop because it was a much more serious disaster (in the sense that more lives were lost) and made a more spectacular picture.

It may sound cold-blooded to talk about loss of human life in this way, but this is unfortunately one of the yardsticks by which the importance of a scoop is measured in the newspaper world. Not that loss of life is an inevitable ingredient of the scoop shot. Indeed, Fleet Street editors would much sooner have a picture of some catastrophic accident in which those involved survived. The miracle escape is happier news than the dismal fatality.

If you think you have a scoop picture, you must ask yourself the following questions.

1   How spectacular is the shot? Two cars colliding at a stock car meeting is hardly news. But if one of the cars crashed into the crowd then you have probably got a scoop.

2 How serious is the incident? In the case quoted above, it would be equally important, in terms of the newsworthiness of the event, if there were injuries or if there were no injuries. The first would be a tragic accident, the second a miraculous escape.

3 How many other photographers have got exactly the same picture? It is usually easy enough to tell this. How many lenses were focused on the subject when the incident took place? If there were several, do they belong to Fleet Street cameramen, freelances or amateurs?

This third question is the most important, because a Fleet Street picture editor with his years of news photograph experience behind him will be in a far better position to judge the drama and value of the picture than you probably are.

So once you have shot the pictures, get to the nearest phone and call the picture desk on a national paper. If you are calling from a distance, reverse the charges. Tell the picture editor what you have taken and where it happened. He will immediately know if he has a staff

photographer covering the event. If it is a serious incident he may already have received a newsflash from one of the press agencies giving him a few details of the event.

If he wants to buy your picture you will have to send him the undeveloped roll of film as quickly as possible. Speed is of the utmost importance with a scoop. A picture which is worth £100 at 4 o'clock in the afternoon may be worth next to nothing 6 hours later. The picture editor will tell you how he wants the film sent to him. If it is a very important story and other means of transport are uncertain, he may send a motor cycle despatch rider to pick it up from you. More likely, he will ask you to send it to his office by taxi, drive it there yourself, or put it on a train. The unprocessed film must be accompanied by a brief note stating what it contains and giving your name, address and phone number. If you have uprated the film, then make a note of that as well, or the newspaper's darkroom won't know how best to develop it. Mark the envelope *To Be Called For* at the terminus concerned. This will

probably be London, but could be either Manchester or Glasgow depending on the nearest printing centre. If you have a very dramatic series of pictures on an important subject, then do not sell all your rights to the material. Tell the picture editor that you want a *percentage of the syndication fees*. If you sell outright you may lose money on an important story because all national newspapers have their own, or are associated with, picture agencies selling their photographs, and those bought outright from contributors, to other newspapers and magazines.

Summary
1   A scoop picture must be exclusive to be worth money.
2   If you think you have a scoop, then DO NOT DELAY a moment. Phone the picture editor on your favourite national paper. Reverse charges if making a long distance call.
3   Tell him what you have got.
4   The price must be fixed by bargaining. The fee will depend on the

importance of the story and the type of picture you have got. Try and fix a minimum fee, with an agreement that he will pay more if the picture is used big, or on a front page or double-page spread.

5   If the editor is not interested, there is nothing to stop you calling another paper and trying your luck. But never sell the same picture on an exclusive basis to two different editors.

6   Send the picture, undeveloped, by the fastest method available.

7   Include your name, address, phone number, a note of what is on the pictures and the ASA rating at which the film was shot.

8   DO NOT waste time by processing the film yourself.

Newspapers in the market for a scoop picture
As a general guide, the highest payment may be expected from the popular press. They are not listed here in any particular order of payment.

Daily Mirror:	Holborn Circus, London, E.C.1. (01-353-0246)
Sunday Mirror:	As above.
Sunday People:	9 Fetter Lane, London, E.C.4. (01-353-0246)
Daily Express:	121 Fleet Street, London, E.C.4. (01-353-8000)
Sunday Express:	As above.
Daily Mail:	Northcliffe House, London, E.C.4. (01-353-6000)
News of the World:	30 Bouverie Street, London, E.C.4. (01-353-3030)
The Sun:	As above.

Payment for scoops
All these papers are interested in buying dramatic action scoops. Payment will vary depending on the importance of the story, the nature of the pictures which you obtain, how much space the photograph occupies and whereabouts in the paper it is used. The following figures should be considered as a guide only. Sometimes they will pay slightly less and on occasions more, possibly on the basis of encouraging other readers to think of them first when they have scoops.
Small inside page use in any of the above: between £35—£75.
Large inside page use in any of the above: between £50—£100.
Centre page spread use of more than one picture: between £100—£500.
Large front page use of one or more pictures: between £100—£500.

Markets for routine action pictures

Local Press
Most local events will be covered by a photographer from the newspaper in whose area they take place. But if there are competitors from different

parts of the country, their local papers are unlikely to send a
photographer. These papers are a good, if low paying, market for
pictures featuring their potential readers. Winning football teams, and
individual successes in everything from athletics to autocross, can find
space in the local press.

Sell : Reproduction rights. If there are a number of papers covering the
same area it is OK to send them each the same picture. Get the addresses
from *Willing's Press Guide.*

Payment : Between £1 and £5 per picture on average.

Marketing notes : You will need to send off the pictures on the day of the
event if they are to stand a chance of inclusion even in weekly papers. At
first you may be content with just a publication and your name

PLATE 86

A local gymkhana is
unlikely to interest the
national press, unless
some celebrity is taking
part. But you may make
sales to local papers,
horse magazines and
the competitors them-
selves if you get good
action shots.

PLATE 87
A dramatic shot at an important match. But such events are usually well covered by newspapers and agencies, as well as full-time freelances. Unless you are very well organised it is pointless to attempt such a coverage – and even then you will be lucky to show a profit unless you get commissions.

underneath it. If you want payment, then state this on the caption. Some local papers think it sufficient to give the photographers a credit line. For some photographers it is sufficient.

House Magazines

If the subject of your picture works for a large company, then the chances are his firm has an internal paper or magazine. You can check by calling them up. If their employee has had a success, they may well buy the picture for inclusion.

Sell : Reproduction rights. You can send a house journal the same print that you sent to the local press. Get address by contacting firm concerned.

Payment : Between £1 and £3 usually.

Marketing notes : If you speak to the editor of the magazine, very often an employee of the firm's public relations or publicity department, you can find out if he is interested and, if interested, will he pay? Some magazines have no budgets for outside contributors.

Specialist Magazines

Britain has more specialist magazines than any other country in the world. Every hobby and interest from yachting and boating to athletics is catered for. You can find a list of these magazines in *The Writers' and Artists' Year Book*, together with a brief outline of their requirements. Generally, they are in the market for single news item pictures and articles illustrated by good photographs.

Sell : Reproduction rights on single news-type pictures. If you send them an article illustrated with several pictures, they will expect to have First Rights on the material; after all, it would be embarrassing for them if they and their rivals both produced identical articles and pictures on the same day.

Payment : News singles between £1 and £8.

Articles from £10 upwards. More for colour.

Marketing notes : Study magazines carefully before sending in long articles. Check that the magazine pays for news pictures. Some rely on local club secretaries to send them these for nothing.

National Magazines.

A dramatic sequence can be worth good money to general magazines like *Weekend* or *Tit-Bits*. See *The Writers' and Artists' Year Book* for others. Their interest will depend less on the event than on the dramatic quality of the pictures.

Sell : First Rights as a general rule. If you have sold the sequence to a local paper, house magazine or specialist journal this may not prevent a sale to a picture magazine for general readers. But you should tell the editor where you have placed it. If a national paper has used one picture from a sequence of shots, this need not prevent a sale of the whole set to a picture magazine. Sometimes, indeed, the picture editor of such a magazine will get in touch with you after seeing the picture in another publication. This may also happen with foreign magazines (see below).

Payment : For a single dramatic black and white picture: between £15 and £25 on average.

For a sequence of black and white pictures: between £40 and £200 on average.

Marketing notes : Market study is essential. If you have colour, then offer them. Colour can increase the fee by 50 per cent or more.

Overseas Magazines

The big picture magazines in Germany, like *Quick*, and *Stern*, and others in France and Italy, are always on the look out for dramatic pictures, preferably a sequence of dramatic shots. If you sell to a British newspaper or magazine, they may contact you direct having obtained your number from the newspaper concerned. All the major European picture magazines have UK-based editors whose job it is to buy photographs. You can approach them yourself, but this is a difficult business for the inexperienced freelance and he or she would do better to have their work handled through an agency (see below).

Payment : For a single black and white, from £25 upwards.

For a black and white sequence, from about £80 upwards.

Marketing notes : There is little point in trying to study a wide range of foreign magazines. The editors look at all the major UK publications and if they like some of your pictures they will certainly call you.

Selling abroad

In my personal opinion, this is best done through an agency. It takes time and considerable marketing experience, plus reliable contacts, to syndicate picture material successfully. Agents will only take your pictures if they think they can make a good return from them. Even if you have sold a set in the UK, a London-based agency may still be prepared to handle your pictures abroad. They will require between 40 and 50 per cent of the fees paid by the magazines for doing so. For their percentage, the agency should make all the necessary prints for syndication and duplicate the colour. They should also turn your notes into a reasonable caption. If you sell through an agent you must be prepared to wait several months for your money.

Colour libraries

These specialise in stocking a vast range of colour material. Clients then come to them with requests rather than their sending out picture material on spec. If they like your work, and this will depend on the quantity, quality and dramatic content which you can offer, they will take you on to their books. You will have to agree to leave your colour with them for a certain period – 2 years on average – and they may never sell anything. But when they do make sales these can be spectacular. An action shot sold for a petrol company promotion, for example, fetched £250. A shot sold to an advertising company for a cigarette campaign made £600. You can find a list of colour libraries in *The Writers' and Artists' Year Book*.

Agents handling action photographs

This is far from a complete list, and consists only of major agencies of which I have personal knowledge. They all enjoy a high reputation in the newspaper world. Potential contributors should get in touch with any agency before sending in work. Increasing overheads mean the agents have to be much more selective in the pictures they handle. Because an agent declines to accept your work it does not necessarily mean that it is too uninteresting or technically poor to sell, only that it will not find a home in sufficient of the big top-paying magazines around the world – these are the markets which these agencies naturally prefer to deal with. Smaller magazines do not pay enough to give an adequate return on the costs of syndicating material. You may still make a handsome profit, because of your far lower overheads, by selling direct to smaller markets.

Camera Press: Russell Court, Coram Street, London, W.1. (01-837-4488)

Colour Library International*: C.L.I. House, Coombe Rd., New Malden, Surrey. (01-942-7781)

Features: 2 Northington Street, London, W.C.1. (01-405-3515)

Keystone: Bath House, 52–62 Holborn Viaduct, London, E.C.1. (01-236-3331)

Picturepoint*: 7 Cromwell Place, London, S.W.7. (01-236-2489)

Rex Features: 25 Gough Square, London, E.C.4. (01-353-4685)

Transworld: 52 High Holborn, London, E.C.1. (01-242-8262)

*Colour only.

PART TWO

In this section of the book you will find concise, practical information about the equipment and techniques required to photograph 25 different action subjects. Of course there are dozens more which it has been impossible to deal with in the space available, but by applying the suggested techniques for covering one subject, you will be able to take successful action pictures at similar events. For example, the equipment and techniques needed to photograph wrestling are very similar to those required for boxing pictures, and the problems involved are the same.

The information should be regarded as a guide rather than a set of rules for covering a particular subject. In photography, only basic, technical rules have to be obeyed; provided you get those right, you are free to discover new, fresh ways of covering familiar action subjects to the limits of your imagination, skill and equipment.

ANIMALS

Equipment

Simple cameras are not very suitable for this type of action work which usually requires a fast shutter speed and longish focal length lenses so that the photographer is able to stand back from the subjects. With domestic animals this is necessary because they are more likely to play naturally if you are at a distance – with wild animals the reasons for long lenses are obvious!

The most suitable lenses for photographing domestic pets with 35 mm. equipment are the 80 mm. or 135 mm. For wild animals, lenses between 135 mm. and 400 mm. will be needed.

Coverage

Pets

Prepare the location in which you are going to shoot your action pictures carefully before bringing in your models. Get the exposures worked out in advance. Select a background which will not be distracting, i.e. flower beds and brick walls make poor backgrounds out-of-doors; wallpaper with a very strong design and chintz chair covers make bad backgrounds indoors. Try and find a background whose tone, on black and white film, will provide a contrast with the tone of the animal. If you have a light-coloured pet, for example, choose a background which will reproduce black or dark grey. Give the animals something to do and let them get on with it. Indoors use electronic flash (bounced) to provide the necessary illumination.

Zoos

Excellent action pictures can be taken in zoos. Feeding time usually provides the greatest activity. Bars and wire mesh can be minimised by using a longish lens (135 mm. on 35 mm. format, for example) at a wide f-stop. This will throw the mesh out of focus and enable you to photograph between the bars. On sunny days, choose a time when the sunlight is such that it does not throw a criss-cross of shadows into the cage. These confuse the image. Use a high shutter speed to freeze the action.

Safari parks

Shooting will have to be done through the car windows, so make certain that the glass is clean. Sit in the back of the car so that you can shoot from either side. Use from 135 mm. to 240 mm. lenses and high speeds to freeze most action, as panning from this position is very difficult.

PLATE 88 (opposite)
A playful lion cub and a long suffering bulldog make an unusual subject that will find ready markets. A 135 mm. lens was used on a Nikon F camera

In the wilds

Long lenses are essential when working in places like Africa and India. A zoom lens can be very useful under these conditions. Take advice from local experts to find the best places from which to take your pictures; often, hides have been constructed for visitors near places such as water holes in the major parks. As light conditions should be excellent, shoot colour whenever possible.
(For full details on animal action photography see my book *All About Photographing Animals and Birds*, Pelham Books.)

ATHLETICS

Equipment
Simple cameras can be used to capture many dramatic action pictures over a wide range of athletic subjects, from running to long jump. Use the techniques described in Chapter Four to capture movement at slow speeds and do not be afraid to experiment with different types of panning and slow speed combinations. Get in as close as possible.

If you can interchange lenses, then use a long focus lens in preference to the standard lens – for example, a 135 mm. focal length lens on 35 mm. format. This will help you throw backgrounds out of focus and slightly compress the perspective to give more dramatic pictures of groups of competitors in track events. A 240 mm. lens, whilst harder to use, will produce even less obtrusive backgrounds and greater perspective compression.

Coverage
When covering running, hurdling or other events involving groups of people, a head-on or 45° angle is often more interesting as it enables you to relate the contestants to one another in a way which is usually impossible with a 90° to camera shot. Furthermore, a sideways shot which includes a number of runners or hurdlers strung out over a distance lacks impact. Use the longer lenses for long jumps too. Pre-focus technique is essential when trying to catch a long jumper with a 135 mm. lens or above. Shots taken from head-on can be more effective than sideways shots as these tend to compress the subject and eliminate distracting foreground and background. Catch the jumper in mid-air or when he lands and throws up the sand. Low angles make the leap seem more impressive.

High jumps can be shot with a wide angle lens, also from a low angle. Watch out for backgrounds when using this type of lens as its depth of field at each stop is so much greater than a long lens. The sky is the best

PLATE 89 (opposite) A head on shot using a long lens to compress perspective can produce effective hurdling pictures. An 800 mm. lens was used on a Nikon camera for this 100 m. hurdles shot. Exposure 1/1000th second f11

PLATE 90
For the hammer throw
a long lens is advisable.
Press the shutter when
the competitor has his
back to you and you
should catch him facing
the camera. Nikon F
camera with 400 mm.
lens. 1/1000th second
f4.5

background. If there are clouds about and you have a yellow filter, try
using this to make the background more dramatic. Watch out especially
for stadium light stands, angles of buildings, telephone lines etc. in the
background of such shots. Remember the value of the diagonal line in
action composition.

When photographing potentially dangerous field sports, such as
hammer throwing, a long lens is advisable. Timing is important for
hammer throwing. If you press the shutter when the player is facing you
on his turn, you will probably only get a shot of his back. Press the
shutter when he has his back to you and you will be more likely to
photograph his front!

Speed guide for athletics

EVENT	SIDE VIEW	HEAD-ON VIEW	THREE-QUARTERS SHOT
Sprinting	1000th sec. With panning speeds down to 1/30th can be used	1/250th – 1/500th	1/500th sec.
Hurdling	Panning not suitable. 1000th sec.	1/250th sec.— 1/500th sec.	1/500th sec. – 1/1000th sec.
Long jump	1/1000th sec. With panning down to 1/60th sec.	1/250th sec.— 1/500th sec.	Poor viewpoint
High jump	Poor viewpoint	1/500th sec.— 1/1000th sec.	1/500th sec.— 1/1000th sec.
Hammer throw	1/500th sec. – 1/1000th sec.	Poor and dangerous viewpoint	1/500th sec.— 1/1000th sec.

Note: With hammer throw the best viewpoint is behind the thrower. A speed of 1/500th second or 1/1000th second will be needed to freeze all movement.

AVIATION

Equipment
As most aviation action photographs will be shot from the ground, long lenses are essential. At air displays where there is low flying and low speed aerobatics, a 135 mm. lens may be sufficient to capture a wide range of action, but it will also be useful to have a longer lens, say a 240 mm. or 400 mm. lens. A motorised camera is useful but not essential (see below for air-to-air remote control shooting) for ground shots.

Coverage
It is better not to work with the camera on a tripod as this anchors the equipment too firmly and you may miss important shots when the unexpected happens.

When shooting black and white, use a u.v. filter to reduce haze, or a yellow filter to produce attractive pictorial effects with clouds and the vapour trails of aerobatic jets. When taking exposure readings, be careful not to under-expose the subject. This is all too easy when photographing a relatively small object against the sky. Do not think

that you must come in close for every shot; very often excellent pictorial action pictures can be taken using a shorter lens—for example, a standard or 135 mm. lens on 35 mm. format – and obtaining a panorama of several machines against the sky. Because the aircraft are likely to be some distance from you, there is no need to use very fast shutter speeds. You will be able to get a wider range of shots at 1/500th second, although jets flying directly across the path of the lens will require a far higher speed to freeze them. Remember that the diagonal line conveys a powerful sense of action, while horizontal lines appear static and tranquil. Use a tilted camera if necessary to produce a sense of speed. At air shows, always be on the watch for the unexpected. Accidents do happen, and if you get a dramatic shot you may be able to sell it for a good price.

Aviation – air-to-air
When shooting air-to-air pictures of aircraft in action, a larger format camera is useful as less enlargement will be needed and camera shake is minimised. A frame finder is almost essential and a u.v. filter useful. If you are hiring an aircraft for air-to-air photography, check the machine out in advance. Some light aircraft are fitted with tinted glass windows and are unsuitable for photography. In others there is no way in which the camera lens can be stuck through the window. If the pilot is agreeable it may be best to remove the door or window section completely so as to give the camera as wide a range of movement as possible, but make certain that you are well strapped in!

When taking your pictures be careful that neither your arms nor hands, nor any part of the camera, rests against a part of the aircraft while taking pictures. The vibrations of the machine will be transmitted to the camera and may cause blur, even at top shutter speeds. Use your body to absorb these vibrations. When using a long lens, make certain that you do not push it out so far that it catches in the aircraft slipstream as this will make it impossible to steady. Air-to-air photography should only be attempted with skilled and experienced pilots. If you are photographing a number of machines in the air at once, make certain that you brief all the pilots about your requirements before take-off. You can tell them what sort of pictures you require and they will tell you whether or not what you want is safe. Radio communication between aircraft is invaluable for air-to-air photography.

Press cameras are bulky to cart around but produce high quality pictures on air-to-air subjects. Probably a 6 cm. × 6 cm. or a 6 cm. × 7 cm. SLR or TLR will provide the best combination of quality and ease of handling. If using a 35 mm. camera, the best lens is probably 105 mm. or a 135 mm. Longer lenses are too difficult to use.

Air-to-air – remote control cameras : As I described in Chapter Seven, motorised cameras can be used to obtain unusual pictures in aviation photography. They can be especially useful in stunt flying as they enable a wide range of spectacular shots to be taken, which would be impossible with any other equipment. These cameras may be mounted on the tail, wing or fuselage of light aircraft by designing and building suitable rigs. The mounting rig must be large enough to distribute the weight of the camera over as wide an area as possible. Thick plywood is best for this purpose. To mount the motorised Nikon on the tail of a Tiger Moth, for example, I used two sections of ½-inch plywood fixed together with high tensile steel nuts and bolts (see Chapter Seven). The most convenient firing button for such an arrangement is a microswitch which can be taped on to the pilot's control column. The camera exposure and focus are, of course, pre-set; when linking the camera to

PLATE 92
For basketball low
angles are generally the
most impressive – they
emphasise the height
of a leap. But do not be
afraid to experiment
with unusual angles.
Here a ladder and two
flash heads (Mecablitz
502 for the key-light
and a Mecablitz 110 on
the camera) have
provided excellent
modelling. Shot by
sports photographer
Bill Smith.

the cabin control be careful that the lead does not foul any of the rudder or flap controls – it goes without saying that the pilot should supervise this operation.

Very wide angle lenses are necessary for this type of picture. A 24 mm. or 28 mm. lens on 35 mm. format is ideal.

BASKETBALL

Equipment
All cameras can be used. One of the best positions is close to the net as this enables you to cover net action and mid-field play. A low angle is

best for net action to emphasise the peaks of action. By capturing the peaks, you can shoot at speeds as low as 1/250th second sastisfactorily.

Coverage
When shooting basket ball indoors, flash will almost certainly be needed. Even if the quantity of the light is sufficient for the shutter speed/f-stop combination required, it is likely that the quality will be too poor to provide crisp, dramatic pictures. A single flash, as I explained in Chapter Six, gives flat illumination and deep background shadows. A better technique is the two-light system with the second flash fired by a slave unit.

BOATING—See Power Boat Racing and Sailing

BOXING

Equipment
When it is possible to get a ringside camera position, then any camera can be used, with electronic flash. SLR cameras may prove difficult to use with flash (see below) but they are still first class when used for available light pictures or with long lenses. For ringside pictures using flash, a camera like a Rolleiflex is excellent.

Coverage
When using SLR's with focal plane shutters to cover amateur bouts, the level of illumination may pose problems. There may not be sufficient light for a high shutter speed exposure, but there will still be enough to produce an image at the fairly slow (around 1/60th second) synchronisation speed of most SLR's. This results in a blurred, ghost image which is distracting, but the problem is overcome by using a camera fitted with a Compur (between-the-lens) shutter and synchronising the flash at a high speed. When using a TLR, the frame finder is essential. Depth of field at small f-stops will take care of focus problems because the area of coverage is so limited.

The majority of boxing pictures are taken from camera positions just below the ring. This is a good vantage point. The low angle gives a dramatic sense of action and the dark background contrasts well with the flesh tones of the boxers when shooting black and white.

When the level of light is high enough to shoot 1/500th second–1/1000th second by available light – even if this means considerable pushing of the film at the processing stage – then you have a much wider range of vantage points. When a bout is being covered by

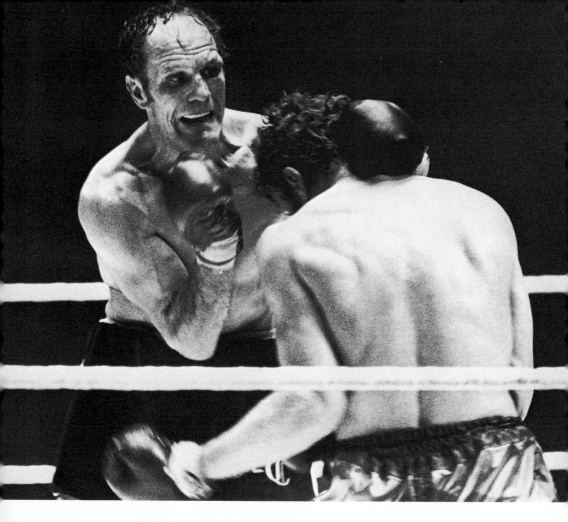

PLATE 93
When the light is strong enough – even if it means uprating the film – available light is best for boxing or wrestling subjects, although you will need more light and higher shutter speeds for wrestling coverage. Henry Cooper in action against Joe Bugner. Nikon F with 400 mm. Novoflex lens. 1/500th second f4.5. Film rated at 800 ASA

television, the extra illumination always makes available light black and white shooting possible. The picture of Henry Cooper and Joe Bugner was taken with a 400 mm. lens from the public seats. The worst position from which to cover both boxing and wrestling is a high angle. This reduces the drama of the action, and the floor of the ring, which is now the background, reproduces a mid-grey that is very close to the flesh tones of the subjects, making them hard to see and reducing the impact of the shot.

CHILDREN

Equipment
All camera types, including simple cameras, can be used. If you have

interchangeable lenses, then an 80 mm. or 135 mm. on 35 mm. format will enable you to get rather more candid pictures.

Coverage
The children must be enjoying themselves and be unaware of the camera if you are going to get spontaneous shots. Give them something interesting to do and then let them get on with it. Remember that confusing backgrounds distract from the subject. Get rid of background out of doors by using a longer than standard lens and opening up the f-stop to limit the depth of field. Indoors, select your background with care; avoid walls with very flowered paper, for example. If you are using flash, bring the subject well away from the background to avoid shadows. The best indoor lighting technique is bounce flash. You can bounce from the wall or ceiling of most rooms without difficulty. If the walls are light, then open up on stop more than you would for direct flash. If using direct flash, have a longish synchronisation lead and direct the light downwards from about 45° to the camera by holding it in your hand. Do not clip the camera to the flash gun and use in this position (see also Chapter Six).

CRICKET

Equipment
This game requires long lenses to cover it adequately; a 400 mm. lens or more will be needed to produce good close-up shots of the wicket. The camera may be conveniently tripod-mounted as all the action takes place within a fairly limited area. If you are keen on cricket and intend to shoot a lot of pictures, it may be worthwhile investing in an old press camera with a roller-blind shutter. Used in conjunction with a roll-film back, this can be quite economical on film. Its main advantage is that it enables you to use long ex-government lenses which were intended for aerial and similar precision work. These tend to be very bulky and heavy, but this hardly matters when the camera can be tripod-mounted – make sure your tripod is a really sturdy model – and, optically, they are often superb. Some of them may not have any aperture control, but you can make one up out of thin metal or stiff card. For black and white work it does not have to be absolutely precise and can be fitted over the front of the lens to avoid having to cut into the lens barrel. Probably, the most suitable f-stops will be f8/f11/f16.

To calculate the diameter of the hole required for a particular f-stop, you need to know the focal length of the lens. Since the f-stop may be simply expressed as the focal length divided by the diameter of the

aperture, working out the size of your f-stops is a matter of simple arithmetic. For example, you have a 800 mm. focal length lens. The diameter of the lens is 95 mm., therefore $\frac{800}{95}$ = f8 (approx.).

To reduce the aperture to f16 we need to cut a mask ($\frac{800}{X}$ = f16, divide 800 by 16=50 mm.) with a hole 50 mm. in diameter. Take some experimental pictures using the home-made f-stops to check your work before an important assignment.

Long lenses may also be lacking lens hoods. The easiest way of making one is to use a tube of stiff black card.

Coverage
The most usual, and probably the best, camera position is head-on to the wicket as this enables most of the main action to be covered. Use a high shutter speed and be fast on the shutter release to catch the moment when stumps fly. When shooting cricket on very bright days, be careful not to over-develop the film as this may create printing difficulties from burnt-out highlight areas. On very contrasty days it may be advisable to rate your film at a lower than recommended speed (i.e. 200 ASA instead of 400 ASA for Tri-X) and then reduce development times in order to cut down the negative contrast. Do not be afraid to try back-lit or side-lit shots. They can be very effective.

CYCLING

Equipment
Cycling photographs can be shot on simple cameras providing you can get in close enough to the subject. With interchangeable lens cameras, wide angle and very long focal length lenses may be used.

Coverage
There are several different types of cycle event; road time trials, track events, indoor 6-day racing and cyclo-cross. Indoor events pose slight problems which can sometimes only be solved with flash. Cyclo-cross often provides the most dramatic pictures. When covering cyclo-cross, try and arrive at the course well before the meeting starts so that you can find the best positions from which to shoot. Natural obstacles such as streams or steep, muddy slopes are likely to provide good shots. The most useful lenses for cyclo-cross are the wide angle, standard and 135 mm. lenses. Watch out for confusing backgrounds, but keep an eye out for dramatic pictorial effects – for example, riders silhouetted against a menacing sky.

For indoor events the best camera position is the centre of the track.

PLATE 94 (opposite) A long lens is needed to provide this type of cricket action shot. An 800 mm. lens on a 35 mm. camera. Exposure 1/1000th second f8. Be careful when processing this type of picture not to push up the contrast

Try panning shots, using speeds down to a $\frac{1}{2}$-second for special effects. The picture will be a blur, but it may convey far more of the action and atmosphere than would be possible with a clinically sharp, flash-frozen shot.

For track events, use long lenses for corner shots to bunch a group of riders dramatically and always be on the alert for spills.

FOOTBALL

Equipment

If you can get a touchline position, close to one of the goals, then almost any of the cameras listed in the first chapter of this book may be used. Slow top shutter speed limitations may be solved by using the techniques described in Chapter Four. Fixed lens TLR's should also be used at the goal area.

PLATES 95–96 (opposite) Two shots by Bill Smith. In the first he has used electronic flash to 'freeze' the movement; in the second he has used a slow shutter speed and panning to produce a shot with far more drama and sense of speed.
PLATE 97 (below) Mid-field shots like this require a long lens. For this picture a 500 mm. mirror lens was used. Exposure 1/1000th second f8

PLATES 98–100 (above, opposite and overleaf) In Rugby football you have a chance of sequence shooting as action develops. Do not be content with a single shot. These were shot on a manual wind camera. Nikon F with 400 mm. Novoflex lens. Exposure 1/1000th second f5.6. Film rated at 650 ASA

If you have to shoot from the public stands, long lenses – at least 400 mm. – will be needed to give you a wide range of action shots. These long lenses are valuable at the touchline positions as well. The Novoflex system is ideal for football coverage, and a motor drive is very useful.

Coverage

As one can see from watching any important match, the goal mouth is the most popular vantage point amongst press photographers. Here you can capture the peaks of the action around the goal mouth and some mid-field play using 240 mm. or 400 mm. lenses. But, when they are allowed alternative vantage points, many sports photographers prefer a centre-line position. Using a 400 mm. lens, they can then cover both goals and all mid-field play. If you are taking pictures for possible publication, make certain that you can identify all the players for your captions. One way of doing this is to take a second photograph after a

tackle or a goal score in order to record the numbers on the back of the shirts for identification.

RUGBY FOOTBALL

Equipment and coverage
The same comments apply. If you have access to the touchline, then all the cameras discussed in the first chapter can be used. Some photographers spend a match sprinting up and down the line after the players. Others prefer a static position near one of the goals. From here, using 400 mm. lenses, they can record mid-field play and tries. It is useful to have two camera bodies, one fitted with a long lens and the other with a wide angle lens, if you are going to work in close to the touchline, otherwise your longer lenses will not be able to focus close

enough to catch the final moment of drama when a try is scored, and there may not be time to change lenses. Alternatively, you can use a long lens well back from the touchline. Motorised cameras are very useful for this type of action subject.

GOLF

Equipment
Simple cameras are not suitable for golf coverage as you will need long lenses to get good close ups without upsetting the players. On 35 mm. format the most useful lenses are from 135 mm. to 400 mm.

Coverage
Driving and putting make good pictures, but some of the most effective

shots are to be found around the bunker as a ball emerges in a blast of sand. Golfers are sensitive to camera shutters, especially when playing in important matches. If you have a 35 mm. range-finder camera, you will be able to work in closer than if you have the noisier focal plane shutter SLR. But with either camera the 135 mm. lens probably takes you as close as you can safely get at a minor match. Use a 240 mm. lens or higher when covering a big tournament with high financial rewards at stake. If you want some special bunker shots, you can always ask a friend or helpful golfer to put on a special performance for you. A shutter speed of 1/1000th second will stop most of the movement, although the end of the club may still be unsharp. But shoot at slower speeds (1/125th second) on bunker shots to catch the blur of flying sand. Look out for pictorial effects too; back or side lighting of sand is effective, and a low angle will make the picture more interesting.

MOTOR RACING EVENTS

Equipment
Pictures may be taken with simple cameras, using panning and 45°-angle techniques, providing it is possible to get close to the subject without taking undue risks. For serious motor racing photography a 35 mm. camera is the best, especially when the equipment has to be carried across rough country (see below). Lenses up to 400 mm. may be used to good effect, and zoom lenses are useful, especially when working with one camera body. For some motor racing and rallying, protection of the equipment from rain and mud will be an important consideration. Use u.v. filters and hoods on all lenses.

Coverage
Study the techniques described in Chapter Four before starting to shoot this high-speed sport. Motor racing is a good subject to gain action experience on as there are a large number of meetings. The RAC publish a handbook of motorsport events which provides information about all races, hill climbs and trials during the season, and many of them are put on by local clubs who will be only too willing to help you get good pictures in return for photographs and/or publicity (see Chapter Eight).

Rallycross
This can produce some very dramatic pictures as the cars speed across rough country. If the course is unfamiliar to you, chat to the drivers. They will know the difficult and dangerous sections only too well! Most

Rallycross can be shot at 1/500th second but 1/1000 second will be needed at times. Use long lenses and avoid taking unnecessary risks.

Formula One Racing

Track passes are usually necessary and these are generally reserved for professionals. But if you are a serious amateur you may be able to talk your way past the marshalls or obtain a pass (see Chapter Eight). If you have to shoot from behind the barrier, don't worry. There are positions on all tracks where you can get dramatic action using long lenses; for example:

Brands Hatch. Good shots can be obtained by catching the cars coming head-on up the hill into the hairpin bend.

Mallory Park. A position on the high bank gives a good view as cars round the bend.

The best positions at other tracks can soon be found after a couple of visits.

Use speeds of 1/1000th second–1/2000th second to freeze side-to-side action. Use panning to put a feeling of action into your pictures. Try some shots at very slow speeds (a $\frac{1}{4}$-second if the light is low enough to permit this long exposure) combined with panning for dramatic effects. This can be especially effective with colour.

Hill Climbs

This produces on average less dramatic material than Rallycross, but can still be worth covering. Watch the cars during practice to see how they take different corners. Pre-focusing can be valuable. Frame up with one car and focus on that spot on the track, then shoot as the next car reaches this point. You can use this technique with all types of motor sports.

MOTOR CYCLE EVENTS – SCRAMBLES/TRACK

Equipment

Simple cameras will only be able to capture a small part of the high-speed action and thrills which these events provide. A 35 mm. camera is easiest to handle and lightest to carry across country. Motor cycle scrambles often take place in winter rain and mud, so protection of camera – and photographer – are important. Use a u.v. filter and a hood on all lenses. Some shots can be captured with standard lenses, but lenses up to 400 mm. may be used to good effect.

Coverage

Mud, especially wet mud, provides a host of spills and many dramatic

PLATE 102
Panning and catching the right moment by using VAT techniques has put movement into this head-on shot of side-car racing. It is the type of picture which editors of specialist magazines and competitors alike will be happy to buy. 200 mm. lens on 35 mm. SRL. 1/500th second f8

shots. Probably the most spectacular pictures can be obtained from the other side of a short, sharp hill when the bikes take off into the air. Standard or 135 mm. lenses are best for this sort of shot, and a motorised camera will enable you to catch a sequence if the rider skids and falls, as frequently happens. Shutter speeds of 1/250th or 1/500 second are sufficient for an action picture of this kind. Shoot from a low angle to make the leap appear as dramatic as possible. At race tracks use panning techniques for side-to-side action. Head-on shots at corners can be effective on dirt track events as the riders spurt clouds of grit under the boots. Use a long lens to compress the perspective and a shutter speed of 1/500th second to put some blur in the flying dirt. Sidecar events provide very dramatic pictures – use a long lens and watch out for the action on corners as the passenger leans right out.

POWER BOAT RACING

Equipment
35 mm. cameras are the most satisfactory when working from another

boat, as the bouncing of the craft makes it very hard to focus and hold the camera. Very long lenses are impossible to handle aboard a speedboat, and 240 mm. is probably the longest practical focal length for boat work. When working from land, lenses of 400 mm. or more must usually be used. Pick your position carefully. Sometimes the best shots can be taken from the harbour jetty or pier at the start of a race, with a standard or 135 mm. lens on 35 mm. format.

Coverage

Protection of the camera when working from a speedboat must be a primary consideration. Keep the neckstrap on at all times, even when changing films. The camera should only be opened under the protection of a cabin or an awning. Use a u.v. filter and a hood on all lenses. Some photographers work with their cameras sealed inside transparent plastic bags. A hole is punched for the lens and the plastic is secured around the lens barrel with a rubber band. If the plastic is thin enough, it is perfectly easy to operate the camera through it. But, provided the camera doesn't actually drop in the water, you will be able to clean off salt spray after the event and leave your equipment none the worse.

PLATE 103
A boat-to-boat shot full of movement, thanks to the low angle and flying foam. Be careful when exposing this type of shot not to be fooled by the light reflected from the water into under-exposing the main part of the subject.

Meter readings must be taken very carefully as the large amount of light being reflected from the water can give too high a reading, especially when you are working with a long lens but using a separate meter. Allow a correction of one f-stop when working on a bright day. Speeds of 1/500th second or 1/1000th second are generally needed to freeze action. Panning can be used on individual boats, but the high-flung spray and the fact that the prow of the boat is leaping from the water is usually sufficient to provide a sense of movement without panning. A yellow filter can enhance the pictorial quality of power-boat shots, not only by putting in clouds but by providing better contrast between the water and the spray. Do not over-develop these negatives if you can avoid it. If the light is good, and at sea you will get a higher reading than under the same lighting conditions on land, underrate fast films (i.e. Tri-X 400 ASA film, rate at 200 ASA) and then cut the development time. Alternatively, use a slower stock in the camera, i.e. Plus-X or FP4. This will reduce the over-all contrast and make it easier to get detail in the sea and spray. FF/DD processing (see Chapter Five) is a good technique for this type of negative.

SAILING

Equipment
Simple cameras are not generally suitable for catching fast sailing action, although you may get some interesting shots as yachts leave the harbour at the start of a race, as long lenses are necessary when working from land. You will get far better pictures working from a boat. The marshall's craft is usually a more stable platform for photography than a sailing boat, but even here you will find it very hard to handle a very long lens, and 240 mm. is probably the longest you will be able to use satisfactorily. Most pictures of yacht and dinghy races are taken from following craft. A recent innovation, pioneered by photographer Alastair Black, has been to use a Nikonos camera fitted with a wide angle lens in the craft itself. A Nikonos is a Japanese-made camera designed mainly for use by skin-divers. It is completely waterproof and needs no extra protective case. It is light and easy to operate with one hand, although distance has to be judged and set visually. Alastair Black has had a special watertight lens housing made for a 21 mm. lens which enables him to work in the cockpit, or actually in the sea, swimming around in a diver's wet suit for protection against the cold. In this way he has produced some highly dramatic shots which are *different*. This can be an important consideration when selling pictures (see Chapters Nine and Ten).

Coverage
Protect the camera and lens as much as possible (see Power Boat Racing above). Use fast shutter speeds (1/500th second–1/1000th second), especially with long lenses under choppy conditions. Use a slow film if the light will allow it, or slightly underrate fast films, then cut the development time. Use a yellow filter for pictorial effects.

SHOWBUSINESS

Equipment
If you are working by the available stage light, you will need a wide aperture lens – around f1.4–f2. You will get most of your action pictures

PLATE 104
One of the off-beat sailing shots taken by Alastair Black using his specialised Nikonos equipment. Getting a different angle on action is important, both for producing more exciting and eye-catching pictures and to improve sales. Nikonos camera fitted with 21 mm. lens in waterproof mount. 1/250th second f8

with a standard or wide angle lens. A slightly long focal length lens (135 mm.) may be useful for portrait shots of the cast.

Coverage

You will probably have to take your shots during the dress rehearsal, but if you can persuade the cast and producer to give you some time for a special photo-call, so much the better. Most stage action can be caught at 1/250th second, but some action, fights, ballet, etc. require 1/1000th second. This will almost certainly mean pushing the film speed (see Chapter Five) but the increased grain will be acceptable if you have got a dramatic picture. When shooting action, have as much light on the stage as possible, though I advise against using flash as this produces very artificial looking pictures. Watch out for backgrounds and use tonal contrast to give your pictures maximum clarity. For example, if two characters are wearing dark clothes and normally say their lines against a black drape, re-position them against a lighter background for your shots, or change your own position to increase the contrast as much as possible. A quiet shutter such as the Leica's is an advantage when photographing a sensitive star or ballet prima donna.

SHOW JUMPING

Equipment

Simple cameras may be used to catch some head-on shots of horses clearing jumps, provided you can get close enough to fill the viewfinder. This is impossible at major events but may be possible at local shows. A zoom lens can be useful, but you will shoot most of your pictures at between 90 mm. and 135 mm. on 35 mm. format when working on fences close to the rails, or from the centre of the arena. Long lenses are not really necessary.

Coverage

Low angles at jumps emphasise the height, but also try some head-on shots using a 135 mm. lens or longer for special effects. Shutter speeds of 1/500th second to 1/1000 second will be needed for sideways or slightly head-on shots, and panning is not possible because it would make the jump unrecognisable. A shutter speed of 1/250th–1/500th second will be sufficient for head-on shots. Use a yellow filter to improve the pictorial quality of your pictures. Timing your shot is critical in show jumping, and it offers an ideal training sport for the action photographer because each type of action is repeated so many times during the event.

SKY-DIVING (PARACHUTING)

Equipment

Camera and lens requirements vary widely for this subject, depending on your position. There are 5 different positions from which sky-diving shots may be taken:

a   *From the ground.* Simple cameras can be used to take the moment as the sky-diver returns to earth, providing you can get in close to him. Otherwise a 135 mm. or 240 mm. lens on 35 mm. format will be needed. High shutter speeds are not necessary and you should get pictures at 1/250th second providing you press the release when the sky-diver is about 20 ft. above the ground.

b   *From another aircraft.* These can be taken with good quality non-interchangeable lens cameras, or interchangeable lens cameras fitted

PLATE 105
A sky-diving picture taken with a motorised Nikon camera fitted to the outside of a Rapide aircraft. It catches the moment as the girl sky-diver falls into space. The panorama of earth gives an impression of her height. Nikon F fired by cable. 1/1000th second f8

with slightly long focal length lenses. The comments on equipment for air-to-air aviation photography apply here.

c *From inside the despatching aircraft.* A motor drive is not necessary here but a wide angle lens is. Because of the cramped conditions in most sky-diving aircraft, a 35 mm. camera is the most convenient.

d *From outside the despatching aircraft.* This requires a motorised camera fitted with a wide angle lens (see below).

e *From a helmet-mounted camera.* Again, this requires a motorised 35 mm. camera for the best results.

Coverage

a *From the ground.* When the sky is used as a background it is impossible to tell whether the sky-diver is 15 ft. or 50 ft. off the ground. A filter can be used to increase the pictorial effect and to give greater contrast between sky and 'chute. Watch out for sudden gusts of wind which can carry the parachutist down on to you – it could be the last thing you ever see! This position is a dangerous one and you will need special permission to stand in the centre of the DZ (Dropping Zone). If several parachutists are landing at once, keep a sharp eye out. Remember that a diagonal line conveys a feeling of movement, so tilt your camera.

b *From another aircraft.* The comments made in connection with air-to-air aviation photography apply here.

c *From inside the despatching aircraft.* The camera can be taken aloft and fired by the photographer. However, such a position is not going to produce really dramatic sky-diving photographs. Once the sky-diver has jumped, he or she vanishes from view in a split-second. A motorised camera is useful to enable you to capture what action can be seen from the cabin. If you are taking this type of picture, make sure you wear a parachute and have some basic training in its use, or strap yourself in well, using a harness which holds you securely but allows you enough movement to get into picture-taking positions.

d *From outside the despatching aircraft.* The camera may be mounted on to the wing or tail of the aircraft (see Aviation) to provide spectacular shots of the moment the sky-divers jump out. Where jumps are being made from aircraft such as the twin-winged Rapide, this is quite a simple operation. The camera, fitted with a wide angle lens, is bolted on to the side of the aircraft wing, pointing back towards the cabin door. From this position it is possible to capture the moments as the parachutist emerges from the aircraft and drops out of sight. The camera can be fired either by the photographer or, if weight problems make it impossible for the cameraman to fly, by the despatcher or last parachutist out of the aircraft.

e *From a helmet-mounted camera.* The final position for the camera is on a helmet bracket. A motorised Nikon is the most frequently used camera for this type of photography. It is a technique which has produced some of the best action sky-diving pictures taken. A wire frame finder extends in front of the sky-diver's helmet visor and the picture is composed by lining up the whole body with the subject. Naturally, such an angle presupposes considerable parachuting skill and can only be attempted by photographers who are also experienced sky-divers. Beginners need all their concentration just to perfect the jump, without bothering about taking pictures.

PLATE 106
A helmet-mounted motorised Nikon F was used to take this air-to-air shot of sky-divers sharing a beer on a dive from 12,000 feet

WATER SKI-ING

Equipment
The only really satisfactory camera and lens to use from the towing boat

is a 35 mm. camera fitted with a 200 mm. lens. With the subject bobbing around at the end of a 70 ft. line, this is not an easy lens to use, but a shorter focal length makes the subject too small on the negative. From the land you will probably need at least a 200 mm. lens to get a sufficiently large image.

Coverage

The points for camera and lens protection already given (see Power Boat Racing) apply to this sport as well. Use a slow film or cut the speed of a fast film and under-develop to reduce contrast. If your negative is very contrasty it will be difficult to hold detail in the water and spray on the print, and unless there is detail in these essential surroundings the picture will look uninteresting. You will need a fast shutter speed – 1/500th–1/1000th second – to freeze the water and the movement of the boat. Slalom races, where the skier weaves in and out of a line of marker buoys, provide more interesing pictures than straight ski-ing.

Technical Glossary

Aperture : The name given to the hole in the diaphram which controls the amount of light passing through the lens. This is denoted by an f-number (i.e. f8, f11, f16). The higher the f-number, the smaller the aperture through which the light can pass. Thus f11 is a wider aperture than f22. In fact, the f-stops progress by either doubling or halving the amount of light they allow to pass through. This means that twice the amount of light can pass through a lens at f8 as can pass, in the same period of time, through a lens at f11. Shutter speeds are arranged in a similar way, with a change from one speed to the next either doubling or halving the amount of time for which the light is allowed to pass through the lens. Thus, by going from a low stop to a higher one (halving the hole through which the light can pass), but at the same time changing from one shutter speed to the next one down (and so giving the light twice as much time to pass through the aperture), you effectively keep the exposure the same. For example, an exposure of 1 second at f8 is the same as 2 seconds at f11. You have halved the size of the aperture, but given the light twice as long to make the journey. Similarly, 1/125th second at f16 is the same as 1/250th second at f11. You have halved the time which the light has to make the journey, but given it an aperture twice as large to pass through. (See also 'Camera'.)

Camera : Whether the camera is the electric Hasselblad which the American astronauts took to the moon, or the box Brownie which you saw in a junk shop for 25p, it has the same basic design. There is a light-tight box with a lens at one end, forming an image on a sheet of light-sensitive material – the film – at the other. The film has a mechanism for moving it so that each picture is made on a fresh area of the material.

Between the lens and the film there is a shutter. This is simply an opaque blind which is moved by springs. It uncovers the lens, allowing light to pass through on to the film, for a fraction of a second. In simple cameras this exposure is likely to be about 1/60th second. The more expensive cameras have a range of shutter speeds, which will probably go down to $\frac{1}{2}$-second and up as high as 1/500th second. On a top-price professional camera you will have a 1-second maximum shutter opening time, and, usually, a 1/2000th second minimum opening time.

The faster the shutter speed, obviously, the less time light has to pass through on to the film. The higher the shutter speed too, the faster the

184 ALL ABOUT ACTION PHOTOGRAPHY

action which the cameraman will be able to 'freeze'. This is important in animal photography because it is often useful to be able to catch some dramatic moment...a dog leaping after a ball, a zoo lion lashing out for his meat and so on. With a simple camera such action may result in a blur on the photograph because the shutter speed is too slow to 'freeze' it.

As we have seen, the higher the shutter speed, the less time light has to pass through the lens. For every photograph there is a correct exposure. This means the amount of light which is needed to produce a good picture. If there is too little light, then the negative will be thin and washed-out looking, and the final print will appear dark and lacking in detail. If too much light falls on the negative, then it will look very dark and opaque, and prints made from it will appear too light with a consequent loss of detail. A correctly exposed negative, on the other hand, will have good detail in both the highlights and the shadow areas. When a print is made from it there will be a range of detail from the darkest to the lightest part of the print, with a pleasant range of mid-tones (greys) between the two. This is what we are aiming for when we expose a piece of black and white film.

Apart from the shutter, which controls the time the light has to pass through the lens, we can control the 'quantity' of light reaching the film by means of an iris diaphram. On a simple camera there may only be one aperture – usually about f11 – which means that, coupled with a fixed shutter speed of, say, 1/60th second, your exposure will remain fixed at 1/60th second at f11. This is an average sort of exposure which the manufacturers have worked out is more likely than not to produce an average result on an average summer day in Britain – the time when, it is assumed, most snaps will be taken. With a fixed exposure you will find your final prints are likely to be too dark when the sun goes behind a heavy cloud, or too light if used by the sea or in snow when the reflective power of the water and snow increases the amount of light.

Aperture controls on a camera enable you to adjust your exposure to match the available conditions. If there is a great deal of light, then you can stop down the lens. The higher the f-number, the smaller the aperture through which light can pass. Each time you go from one number to a higher number, you halve the amount of light passing through the lens. That means that if 100 units of light reach a piece of film at f8, then 50 will reach it at f11 and 25 at f16. (See also 'Aperture' above.) So the second thing you buy with a more expensive camera is a greater range of aperture controls.

But the main thing you pay for in any camera is the lens. On a cheap camera the definition of the lens is likely to be poor. This will make it difficult to produce sharp enlargements of your pictures. A simple camera may also have a fixed focus. This means that without a special additional lens you will be unable to take pictures closer than about 6 ft. At a distance of 6 ft. you will probably cover a fairly wide subject area, perhaps being able to photograph a person as far down as the waist. This means that small objects – kittens and puppies, for example – photographed from the minimum distance will produce a very small image on the negative area. Further, because of the quality limitations of the lens, you won't then be able to enlarge the negative to bring up the portion of the picture which you want.

In addition to having a high definition, a better quality lens will usually have a wider maximum aperture. On a fairly cheap camera the lens will probably have a maximum f-stop of about f3.5. This will make it almost impossible to use under low light levels if a fairly high shutter speed is required. Too little light will reach the negative and the final print will be too dark.

Chemical fogging : See 'Fogging'.

Compur shutter : See 'Diaphragm shutter'.

Dark slide : A light-tight wooden or metal slide which contains a sheet of cut film or, in the old days, a glass plate. Many dark slides will take 2 sheets of films or plates and are known as 'double-dark' slides. A thin metal or plastic sheath is removed to load the slide and again when the dark slide has been fitted into the camera in order to make the exposure.

Depth of field : The range of distance in front of and behind the point of focus which is rendered acceptably sharp on the film. Depth of field varies according to the f-stop being used and the focal length of lens. The smaller the f-stop, the greater the depth of field. The longer the focal length of a lens, the shorter will be its depth of field at any f-stop. This is one reason why long lenses, frequently used in action photography, are difficult to focus.

Depth of focus : The distance through which the film may be moved without an image of a flat object becoming unsharp. The smaller the f-stop, the greater the depth of field. When enlarging, slight errors in focusing the enlarger lens may be corrected by depth of focus as you stop down. Similarly, a small stop on the camera lens will help correct minor errors in focus.

Development : The action of a developing agent on black and white film is to convert silver halide salts into metallic silver in direct proportion to the amount of light which has fallen on them. Highlight areas are therefore converted to metallic silver (making them dark) far more than shadow areas. When the negative is printed this process is reversed. The dark areas on the negative protect the bromide paper from the light, so only a small amount of silver halide reduction takes place. Shadow areas, on the other hand, provide less screening for the enlarger or contact printer lamp and so considerable conversion of the silver takes place in the paper. Thus highlight areas in the original scene are reproduced as light areas on the final print, while shadows in the original scene are reproduced as dark areas on the final print.

If the black and white negative has been under-exposed, some correction can be made during processing by extending the developing time or using a higher developing temperature to speed up the reduction of the silver halides. This is known as 'forced' or extended development.

Diaphragm : A variable hole in a piece of metal which controls the light passing through a lens. Most cameras are fitted with iris diaphragms – thin leaves of metal which can be adjusted to any diameter hole required.

Diaphragm (Compur) shutter : A shutter built between the lens elements. Thin metal leaves open and close with speeds ranging from 1 second to 1/500th second. Because the leaves open completely, the speed being changed merely by their rate of opening and closing, flash can be triggered at high shutter speeds. This is not the case with focal plane shutters (see below). For this reason, diaphragm or Compur shutters are useful for synchro-sunlight photography.

Electronic flash : A brief and brilliant flash of light produced by an electric discharge in a gas-filled tube. The same tube can be used for many thousands of flashes, but the initial cost of the unit is high. A capacitor, or series of capacitors, are used to store the high voltage produced from the mains or from a battery. Because they operate at a high voltage, care should be taken when using the larger guns in wet conditions.

Exposure meter : A device for measuring the amount of light, either falling on the subject (known as taking an incident reading) or being reflected from the subject. There are two types of meter. One uses a selenium cell to produce electricity in proportion to the amount of light falling on it, and this is then measured by a sensitive meter. But, because the hairspring of the meter's needle has a certain inertia, which must be overcome before the pointer can move at all, this type of meter will not function in very low levels of light. For this reason many photographers prefer a cadmium sulphide meter. Here the cell resists electricity, supplied from a built-in battery, in proportion to the light falling on it. Because there is usually electricity flowing in the circuit to overcome the inertia of the needle, these meters are capable of operating under much lower light conditions.

Film speed : Each film has a sensitivity to light denoted by a figure which is printed on the box containing it. This is usually quoted as ASA (American National Standards Association) and then a number, as well as DIN (Deutsche Industrie Norm) and then a number; and sometimes you see a BSI figure quoted (British Standards Institute). For example, Tri-X film is normally rated at ASA 400.

f-number : A figure which denotes the size of the aperture being used. Exposures must be quoted in terms of f-stop and shutter speed.

Filter factors : See 'u.v. filter' below.

Flash factor : Manufacturers of electronic flash guns and flash bulbs provide a guide number which enables the correct f-stop (when using flash direct) to be calculated. The flash factor varies with the film speed – the faster the film, the higher the number. To obtain the f-stop, it is only necessary to divide the distance (from the flash source to the subject) into the guide number. For example: Guide Number (Flash Factor) 160. Distance from lamp to subject 20 ft. $160 \div 20 = 8$. The correct f-stop is, therefore, f8. If you need to work at a particular f-stop, you can discover the correct working distance for the lamp by making a similar division into the Guide Number. For example: Guide Number 200; f-stop required f16. $200 \div 16 = 12.5$ ft.

Focal lengths : The distance from the centre of the lens (actually from a point known as the nodal point) to the plane at which it will focus on an object at infinity. This means a 50 mm. lens will form an image of an object at infinity at 50 mm. (5 cm.) from its nodal point.

Focal plane shutters : Metal or fabric blinds which operate just in front of the film, almost at the focal plane of the lens, hence their name. They are capable of much higher top speeds than the diaphram shutter – 1/1000th second and more – because their speed is adjusted in two ways. One, by increasing the speed at which the blind travels across the film, and, two, by making the slit in the blind smaller. At high speeds – above 1/125th second in most cameras – the exposure is made by a slit passing across the film and exposing it in stages. Because of this, it is not possible to synchronise electronic flash much above 1/60th second. You can, however, use special focal plane flash bulbs. These are designed to burn for a period of time sufficient to give an even exposure across the whole width of the negative area.

Fogging : An over-all increase in density due to one of two causes: *Light fogging :* If film is exposed to light, other than through a camera, over-all but not necessarily uniform fogging changes take place in the emulsion. On processing, this results in a grey 'fog'-like cast which clogs up highlight areas and obscures shadow detail. Minor fogging may not make the negative unprintable but it will reduce definition and print quality. Major fogging, as would be caused if the light were switched on after a film had been loaded into a processing spiral, might ruin the film. *Chemical fogging :* The appearance of chemical fogging is similar to light fogging, but it is caused by increased development times producing an over-all conversion of silver halides in the emulsion to silver. Most developers designed to give high film speeds contain an anti-fogging agent. Minor chemical fogging is not serious, although it will reduce definition, flatten the negative contrast and increase grain size.

Grain : A negative image consists of particles of black, metallic silver. The more these particles clump together, the coarser the image and the more grainy the print made from the negative. Increasing development times causes the silver particles to clump. By using a fine-grain developer, you can reduce the clumping. However, it is important, if developing for a very fine-grain result, to keep all the processing chemicals at the same temperature – this includes the final wash.

Silver halides : The silver salts used in a photographic emulsion to produce the image.

U.v. filters : A filter designed to cut down ultra-violet light. It is useful in reducing haze when taking pictures at sea, or in the mountains. Its primary use in action photography, especially in the field, is to reduce the risk of dirt and damage to the lens surface. No exposure correction is necessary when using a u.v. filter. With all other filters (yellow, enabling clouds to be photographed, for example) an increase in exposure is necessary due to light loss passing through the filter. Every filter has a filter factor. If the factor is ×2, then the film must be given twice the exposure indicated by the meter if the filter is fitted.

Index